D0310444

Counterstrike
Entebbe

COUNTERSTRIKE ENTEBBE

Tony Williamson

COLLINS
St James's Place, London
1976

William Collins Sons & Co Ltd
London · Glasgow · Sydney · Auckland
Toronto · Johannesburg

First published 1976
© Tony Williamson 1976

ISBN 0 00 216138 9

Set in Monotype Times
Made and Printed in Great Britain by
William Collins Sons & Co Ltd, Glasgow

For Lieutenant-Colonel Yonatan Netanyahu
and for all those who died at Entebbe

Contents

Maps and Plans

Foreword

I began my research in Israel some three days after the assault on Entebbe, interviewing hostages, soldiers, ministers and generals. I realized very soon that this remarkable story called for a narrative style which would capture the immediacy, the emotions and most of all the drama of one of the most audacious rescue operations of our times.

The narrative style I chose does, I believe, give this sense of immediacy. However, in every case the dialogue used is as accurate as the memories of those people who recalled it for me. The information contained in the first chapter was gathered from various sources, particularly the Israeli Intelligence Service, which was most helpful. The remainder of the story, put together piece by piece during my stay in Israel, is a full account of what really happened in Uganda, Israel, and on Flight 139. Some of this information has been classified as secret in Israel on the grounds that similar tactics could be used again. However, I am far from convinced of the validity of this reasoning and the only information I have deliberately omitted concerns diplomatic activities which, though interesting, could cause acute embarrassment to certain governments. I did accept the Israeli military policy on the use of individual names, with the exception of certain senior officers, and have not therefore used the names of soldiers, technicians or doctors involved in the operation.

I have endeavoured to be impartial. If anything, before I started I knew more about the aims and methods of the PLO and PFLP than of the Israelis, and certainly my research into the Baader Meinhof for a previous book gave me an insight into the attitudes of Boese and Tiedemann. Nevertheless, as the full picture of Operation Entebbe emerged, I began increasingly to admire the spirit behind the operation.

The Israelis have an implacable logic, a courage that is based on the cold realities of life rather than the illusions of an ideal. But what left me with a sense of awe was the energy required by this small nation to mount such a complex and audacious operation in such a short space of time, and in the certain knowledge that 'official' world opinion would condemn their action.

Israel's Minister of Defence, Shimon Peres, put it very simply when I asked him if he had expected so many world governments to react in the way they did.

'If we had handed over the prisoners,' he said, 'everyone would have understood, but few would respect us. If we went and rescued our people, everyone would respect us . . . but few would understand.'

After talking to so many people in Israel I believe I understand. For that reason this book is dedicated to Sgan-Aluf Yonatan (Yoni) Netanyahu, a brave young man who died at Entebbe and who personified, in every way, the spirit of the people of Israel.

Cheshire, England   TONY WILLIAMSON

Chapter 1

It began in the gleaming modern city of Kuwait on Sunday, 27 June, when three men and a woman met in an apartment in the early hours of the morning. It was almost dawn, and soon the cries of muezzins would sound from the ornate towers of the mosques. But the call to prayer, as the sun rose over Mecca in the East, held no interest for the four people in that room. They were concerned with more violent things. Hundreds would die, directly or indirectly, as a result of the plan they were now discussing.

The leader of the group was a German lawyer called Wilfred Boese. He was 28 years old, fair-haired and tall with penetrating blue eyes. He spoke in a firm, quiet voice as though violence was not a part of his life, and yet in the past few years he had emerged as one of the leading anarchists in the Baader Meinhof movement. He was an associate of Carlos, 'the Jackal', Ramirez, one of the world's most wanted men, and in 1975

1

he had planned the bazooka attack on an El Al flight at Orly Airport.

Boese was an intelligent man with a smooth and persuasive manner which had attracted the attention of Carlos Ramirez in 1974, when the South American was forging links between the Popular Front for the Liberation of Palestine (PFLP) and the Baader Meinhof group. In 1975 Carlos recruited Boese into the Palestinian organization as part of his policy of creating a united terrorist movement which would support anarchists throughout the Western world. This movement, known secretly as the 'Refusal Front' from its rejection of the laws of Western society, was actively extending its influence throughout 1975 and 1976 in such organizations as the Red Aid in Holland, the IRA, the Red Army in Japan, the Dormo in the Yemen, the South American arm of the PFLP and the Tupamara in Chile. It was particularly successful in establishing sympathetic support within the African continent and, through the efforts of Dr Waddie Haddad, was strong in Libya, Somalia and Uganda.

The activities of the French and German governments, and their support of Israel, made them natural targets for the PFLP. It was also important, for strengthening the reputation of the Refusal Front, that a major blow should be struck which would force these governments to release from prison members of the Baader Meinhof, the PFLP and Black September, and the Japanese Red Army terrorist, Kozo Okamoto.

In May 1976, when Ulrike Meinhof was found hanged in her cell in Germany at the height of the controversial trial of Meinhof and Andreas Baader, Boese began to train for the hijacking of an airliner. His team was composed of two Palestinians from Kuwait and 24-year-old Gabrielle Kroecher-Tiedemann.

Tiedemann was a dark-haired girl with a round face, stocky figure and an abrasive manner. She joined the Baader Meinhof movement as a teenager and knew Ulrike Meinhof before Ulrike was finally arrested by West German police. Tiedemann became one of the leaders of the anarchist movement and took part in the attack on the Opec ministers in Vienna. This became her passport into the PFLP ánd, in 1976, she moved to the Middle East and became known by the Turkish code-name of Kalimiri.

She had an arrogant, even brutal manner and was rarely seen without a pistol. Death was no stranger to her and she boasted about killing a policeman in Vienna.

Throughout May and June she had trained with Boese and the two PFLP Arabs in Kuwait, rehearsing the moment when they would take control of the airliner and the route they would then follow. Meetings had also taken place in Benghazi with the South American who would take command of the actual operation.

His name was Antonio Degas Bouvier. He was a tall, rather handsome man with a neat moustache and stylish clothes. He was very close to Carlos, the Jackal, and had accompanied him to London in the bid to assassinate Edward Sieff, the Jewish head of Marks and Spencer, the British department store chain. Bouvier had also taken part in planning the kidnappings at the Munich Olympics and was a key member in the newly emerged Refusal Front. Together with Dr Waddie Haddad, the political director of the hijacking who would operate from Mogadishu in Somalia, Bouvier had evolved a plan which appeared to be foolproof.

The key to it was President Idi Amin. He was already a declared sympathizer of the Palestinian cause with PFLP bases in Uganda, and even his personal guards were Palestinian. In exchange for protection and operating facilities at Entebbe, the Ugandan president would be given the role of mediator.

It was the kind of theatrical performance that President Amin would find irresistible. On the one hand he could indulge in the sympathetic role of negotiator, with all the attendant press conferences that would inevitably follow, whilst on the other he could enjoy the spectacle of Israel begging for assistance. His prestige, at the height of the conference of the Organization for African Unity, of which he was President, would be enhanced enormously.

It was an offer that Idi Amin could not refuse, and his agreement would place the hostages more than 2000 miles from Israel in a hostile country ruled by a man who used rape, torture and murder with no more compunction than other governments used parking tickets. His well-equipped army of more than 20,000 troops made Uganda the perfect setting for the PFLP's coup.

Bouvier was supremely confident of success. 'Our plan is foolproof,' he told Boese and Tiedemann. 'By the time the Israelis are aware of the hijacking we will be in Libyan airspace and secure.'

He told them that once they were in Entebbe there would be no way that Israel could intervene. Their people would be 2000 miles away, in a hostile country. Between would be Libya, Egypt, the Sudan and Saudi Arabia. The Israelis would be powerless and eventually be forced to negotiate. The initial time limit would be 72 hours, but this would inevitably be extended. It was, in fact, in their interests to delay negotiations and extend deadlines. With success guaranteed, the publicity would help to counteract the damaging news coming out of the Lebanon.

The importance placed on the operation by the PFLP was illustrated by the key people involved. Together with Bouvier, there was also Haj Faiz Gaber, the guerrilla chief who helped form the PFLP with George Habash, and the head of the Operations Branch, 43-year-old Abdel Latif Razag. These three men would be waiting at Entebbe when the hijacked airliner arrived and would be in constant touch with Dr Waddie Haddad, another founder of the PFLP, in Somalia.

After the meetings in Benghazi, where it was arranged that the captured airliner would refuel before flying on to Uganda, Boese and Tiedemann returned to Kuwait and finalized their plan for boarding the aircraft. The Arabs would be known only as 39 and 55, and Tiedemann as number 10.

In the early hours of 27 June, they left the apartment in Kuwait and drove to the International Airport to board a flight scheduled to arrive at Athens at 7 a.m. The Germans travelled together, buying first-class tickets for Paris. The two Arabs arrived at the airport separately, each carrying a tin of dates which contained two 7.65 mm Czech automatic pistols and two

6

grenades. They travelled tourist and, on arriving at Athens, went straight into the departure lounge as transfer passengers. In this way they avoided the normal security check which would almost certainly have led to the examination of the tins of dates.

Boese and Tiedemann, who was now wearing a blonde wig, waited in the international departure lounge until the passengers began to board Flight 139 for Paris. The aircraft, on its way from Tel Aviv, was carrying more than a hundred Israelis. Shortly before boarding, Boese went to the men's toilet and was joined by the Arab now known as 55. Once they were alone the Palestinian transferred the pistols and grenades to Boese, who then returned to Tiedemann.

As they walked casually on to the Air France airbus, Tiedemann had two grenades and a pistol in her handbag, and Boese an automatic pistol in his pocket. Behind them, going into the tourist class cabin, were the two Arabs carrying their tins of dates.

It was the morning of 27 June, and operation Entebbe was about to begin.

Chapter 2

Captain Michel Bacos lifted his Air France airbus away from Athens International Airport and turned on to his course over the shimmering Aegean for Paris. On board were a crew of 12 and 258 passengers, the majority of them from Israel. According to his chief stewardess they were in a boisterous mood. The weather was perfect and, completing his final check, he handed over to his co-pilot.

In the first-class cabin a stewardess was serving drinks. One of the passengers was a woman wearing a dark blue skirt, a light blue blouse, and blue stockings. She had a box of chocolates on her lap and spoke with a guttural German accent. The stewardess had reason to remember the woman. When she had boarded the aircraft at Athens with a young German man, some of the first-class seats had been occupied by passengers from the crowded tourist section. Although there had never been any likelihood of her being refused a seat in the first-class cabin, the woman had immediately become furious. In spite of attempts to calm her down, she had angrily ordered an elderly Jew out of a seat. Her manner was harsh and arrogant to the point of being offensive.

Itzhak David, deputy chairman of the Miriat Bialik council in Tel Aviv, had watched the incident with increasing anxiety. The woman was behaving in an extraordinary manner, as though the two seats were a matter of life and death for her and the young man. The arrogance in her manner and the uneasy look of warning that the fair-haired man gave her, made him wonder if there was not some deeper motive for her actions.

Itzhak sat and thought about it as the airbus took off, deciding finally that his uneasiness began when he saw two Arabs board the plane. There had seemed to be something unnatural about their movements. He looked again at the German couple, wondering, deciding finally that perhaps he was wrong.

The stewardess was passing out drinks at the rear of the compartment when Tiedemann rose to her feet and stepped into the aisle. With legs straddled, arms held high above her head, she shouted for attention. With a chill of horror the stewardess saw that in each hand she held a grenade.

'Sit down,' she ordered. 'Everyone must sit down.'

At that moment the tall, well-dressed German with fair hair walked up the aisle, waving a pistol at the stewardess, and entered the flight deck. From the tourist section there were screams and shouts from passengers.

Sarah and Uzi Davidson were among the passengers in the tourist section. With them were their two children, Ron aged sixteen, and Benjamin aged thirteen. The children were playing gin rummy with their mother when the first woman screamed. At first Sarah thought it must be someone who was airsick, but as she tried to look over the seats in front of her other women began to scream hysterically.

Uzi had the seat by the aisle and Sarah asked him what was going on. His expression when he turned to her made her suddenly feel afraid. He was beginning to shake his head, as though he could not believe what he was seeing, when two men ran up the aisle towards the first-class cabin. One man had a yellow shirt, the other a red one. With numbed disbelief she saw that they had pistols in their hands.

'We are being hijacked,' she said. 'They are hijacking us.'

Uzi Davidson was a quiet, phlegmatic man in his late thirties. He worked as a commercial engineer and lived contentedly with his family in a flat in Ramat Aviv. The trip to France was a very special and proud thing for Uzi. The holiday was a gift to his son who had never been abroad and would next year begin military service. It was also a Barmitzvah present for Benjamin, perhaps the most important gift from a Jewish father to his son.

For Uzi it was all suddenly going dreadfully wrong. At the head of the aisle the man in the red shirt was waving his pistol at screaming passengers, whilst the man in the yellow shirt was pushing a stewardess into the first-class cabin. He looked down at his son, Benjamin, and found him gazing back with terrified eyes. The boy began to sob, saying again and again. 'I don't want to die.'

Sarah gathered Benji in her arms and Uzi told them all to crouch down in their seats as far as they could. They stayed that way for a few minutes until passengers began to file down from the first-class cabin, pushed by the two Arabs in bright shirts and a woman in blue who kept waving a grenade and pistol and shouting for everyone to shut up and sit down.

Sarah searched in her bag and found a bottle of valium tablets. She made the children take one and then took one herself. Over the intercom there came the announcement they had all been dreading.

'We are Palestinians,' said the voice. 'If you remain seated and do as you are told no one will be harmed.'

The message was repeated again, then the speaker began to give instructions to the hijackers whom he referred to as comrades 55, 39 and 10. The two Arabs, now carrying two boxes of chocolates, began to tie them on the emergency exits. They warned passengers nearby that the boxes contained explosives which would be detonated if there was trouble.

The intercom was switched on again and a man's voice with a heavy German accent told them: 'My name is Ahmed el Kubesi of the Gaza Strip Che Guevara commando unit of the Popular Front for the Liberation of Palestine.'

He then spoke for ten minutes, telling them that the aircraft had been hijacked because this was the only way to convince Israel that the rights of the Palestinians were greater, both historically and morally, than the rights of the Jews. He informed the now silent passengers that they were to be held as hostages for the release of many freedom fighters presently in prisons in Israel and Europe. They bore no personal animosity towards the hostages, he said, and they would be in no danger as long as they obeyed orders.

12

For Sarah Davidson it was not an assurance that carried much conviction. On either side of the aircraft were the boxes of explosive, in the hands of the two Arabs were pistols which seemed about to go off at any moment, and walking up and down the aisle was a woman with sharp, cruel features who appeared to enjoy the fear on the passengers' faces when they saw the grenade in her hand.

If this was not being in danger, Sarah thought, then she did not know what was. For a brief while she became convinced that they were all doomed, that the terrorists were going to blow up the aircraft in the sky.

Further along the cabin a child of six was asking his mother with tragic eyes if it would hurt when he died. His mother could only hug him to her and try to hide her tears. Towards the rear of the tourist section another woman had begun to cry hysterically. She was British and her name was Patricia Heyman. Since the hijack had occurred she had begun to feel pain in her abdomen and it was getting worse. The problem was, Patricia Heyman was six months pregnant.

On the flight deck Boese stood over the captain and crew with his pistol cocked, ready for any resistance. The captain, however, had already made it clear that for the safety of the passengers – his primary concern – he and his crew would co-operate with the hijackers and offer no resistance. Below them was the main runway of Benghazi Airport, the control tower already guiding them in for the landing.

The Air France airbus was refuelled at Benghazi and prepaied to take off immediately on the last and longest leg of its journey. On board there was a brief delay, a conference between Tiedemann and Boese in which she told him that the pregnant woman on board had begun to haemorrhage and that keeping her would present problems later. Boese agreed that she should be left in Libya and told one of the crew to inform Benghazi control tower of their decision. The arrangements and discussions with the Libyans took most of the afternoon and evening. It was nine houis before the airbus finally took off for Uganda, leaving Mrs Patricia Heyman in an ambulance on her way to hospital.

In the aircraft the passengers had begun to wonder where they were going and what kind of help, if any, would be available to them. The leader of the terrorists had announced through the public address system that they were now heading for their final destination, and to many this meant a brief journey to one of the Arab countries. Everyone had begun to speculate on which country this would be, a considerable body of opinion being that Beirut was the logical

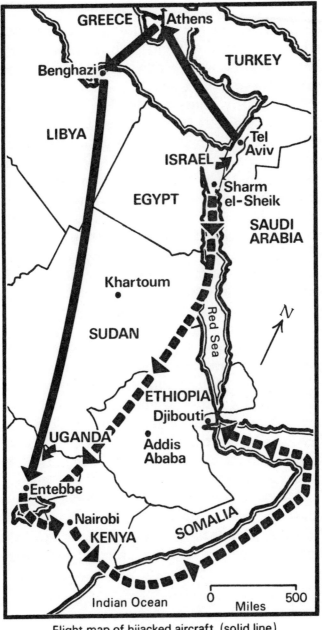

GREECE • Athens

Benghazi

TURKEY

LIBYA

Tel Aviv

ISRAEL

EGYPT

Sharm el-Sheik

SAUDI ARABIA

Khartoum

Red Sea

SUDAN

N

ETHIOPIA

Djibouti

UGANDA

Addis Ababa

Entebbe

SOMALIA

Nairobi

KENYA

Indian Ocean

0   500
Miles

Flight map of hijacked aircraft (solid line)
and assault force (broken line)

destination. The wildest guess was China. But no one imagined in that first hour after leaving Benghazi they were heading across Libya and the Sudan towards Uganda.

In the early hours of Monday morning, the Air France airbus skimmed over Lake Victoria and touched down at Entebbe. Inside there was jubilation as Boese announced over the loudspeakers that they were now in Entebbe where the Ugandan people would help them. He spoke quietly, in a soothing voice, and many of the passengers believed that he was telling them their ordeal was over. When he finished speaking people began to clap, some crying with joy. It seemed obvious that the hijackers had agreed to release the hostages, or had come to some acceptable arrangement with Israel.

For young Nadia Israel it was an enormous relief. Nadia was seventeen, a slim, pretty girl with long black hair and shy brown eyes. She was travelling with her aunt, 21-year-old Nina Zrehen, and had desperately been trying to hide her fear. Now, at last, the nightmare seemed to be over and she began to applaud enthusiastically with the other passengers.

Outside the aircraft a Ugandan service vehicle delivered cartons of soft drinks and the Arab hijackers gave these to the stewardesses to pass out to the passengers. Everywhere people were beginning to relax, to smile again.

Gradually the smiles became strained. There was no move to let them off the plane and the heat built up inside. And something else was worrying Nadia. The German woman, number 10, seemed relaxed and triumphant. When she spoke to the two Arabs they were laughing together, as though they had nothing at all to fear.

After hours of discomfort and dwindling hope the doors were opened and the passengers told to disembark. It was then, for the first time, that they came face to face with the grim reality of the 'help' that Uganda was going to give them.

A cordon of soldiers surrounded the aircraft with automatic rifles. From the doorway a double line of Ugandan soldiers faced inwards, watching the 257 passengers stream out towards the old terminal building. At first it seemed as though the guns were there to protect them, but then as Boese and his group emerged from the airbus soldiers moved towards them, slapping their backs, laughing, kissing and embracing the terrorists.

The dejected line of passengers watched and faced the truth. The guns held by the Ugandans were not pointing at the hijackers . . . they were pointing at them.

Chapter 3

In Jerusalem an emergency session of the Knesset, Israel's parliament, was under way. With grave features Prime Minister Yitzhak Rabin informed the house that the government could expect to receive an ultimatum from the hijackers. He believed that Israel above all was the target of the terrorist action. If it failed to comply with the demands that would be made then it would be Jewish hostages that would be killed.

The leader of the opposition, Menahim Begin, was the first to speak in reply to the Premier. He told the house that this was not a time for party politics or for rhetoric. It was a time for unequivocal support for the government and its ministers and he spoke for all parties in condemning the hijacking and offering the fullest co-operation with the government in this tragic hour.

The responsibility for any action or countermeasure taken by the government fell squarely on the shoulders of two men. They had spent the previous day at Tel Aviv's Ben Gurion Airport, following the course of the hijacked aircraft until finally it had landed at Entebbe. For the first few hours they had wondered if, after refuelling at Benghazi, it would return and land in Israel to present the ultimatum.

There was no doubt in the minds of Defence Minister Shimon Peres or the Chief-of-Staff, General Mordechai Gur, that they were being presented with a situation which had no parallel with previous hijacks. The hostages were being held in a hostile country where the hijackers were clearly being assisted by the President and his army.

Any action against the hijackers must, therefore, also be an action against Uganda. The consequences of this would be formidable, and yet the Minister of Defence had no hesitation in asking General Gur to consider the possibility of military action.

The two were close friends, both professionally and socially. This rapport was now vital if they were to co-ordinate an operation which would have to overcome many obstacles, both political and military.

In the early hours of Monday morning, about two hours after the touch-down at Entebbe, they met in Shimon Peres's office in the Ministry of Defence building, the Kiryah, in Tel Aviv. The building was part of the Military Headquarters complex, an eight-storey block with pebble-dashed walls set amidst palm trees and eucalyptus. General Gur's office was in the connecting building, but could be reached along a short stretch of corridor.

Together they studied maps and intelligence reports in the minister's large, air-conditioned office with black panelled walls. There were potted palms around the room, black leather chairs and glazed chunky ashtrays. Behind the large, black desk was a wall map covering the area between Israel and Northern Africa as far as Ethiopia and Uganda.

Reports confirmed that the hijacking was the work of George Habash's Popular Front and that the director of the operation, Waddie Haddad, was one of the most militant enemies of Israel. Haddad, they knew, had connections with the Baader Meinhof through Bouvier, and early reports that the man and woman in charge of the hijacking were German were already being accepted by Israeli Intelligence as proof that this was a major terrorist operation.

General Gur was Chief-of-Staff because, in addition to his vast experience, he had qualities of logic and realism which enabled him to assess situations without emotion. He had surrounded himself with commanders of great vitality and imagination, but he preferred himself to be the sobering influence. He was always conscious of his early days as commander of the country's first paratroop battalion, and he knew all too well the unlimited courage that seemed to be so much a part of the Israeli military tradition.

Many of the men in that battalion, including himself, had been drawn from the old Unit 101, the first commando unit whose members became known as 'The Guys'. When this unit was absorbed into the paratroop brigade its spirit infected the entire battalion. Its exploits in the Israeli wars since the 1960s are legend.

General Gur knew how easy it was to rush into battle and rely on courage and ingenuity to win the day, but there also had to be a steadying influence, the cold assessment of odds. When he looked at the map he saw Egypt, Libya, the Sudan and Ethiopia lying between Israel and its objective. To cross that area with a force large enough to guarantee success would alert countries who would quickly go to the assistance of the hijackers and Uganda. The result of that would be disastrous.

He called in his Second-in-Command, Major-General Yekuti Adam, and the Air Force Commander, Beni Peled. For an hour they assessed all the available information, considered distances, transportation, the military strength of the Ugandans at the airport. There was no doubt in the minds of General Gur's deputy commanders that an attack was feasible, but this was not enough for the Chief-of-Staff. He wanted facts, figures and a plan.

Shimon Peres strode around the office, gesturing at the map, at the city of Tel Aviv outside. They must present the government with a military option, he declared. If this was not done there would be no alternative but to capitulate to the demands of the terrorists and this would, in the future, cause incalculable damage. With 53 of the world's most dangerous terrorists loose, there would soon be a hundred Entebbes. No one in that room believed that the terrorists who were released would go home to live a quiet and peaceful life. They would be out for revenge, more determined than ever to strike at Israel.

'If we cannot find a workable plan,' Shimon Peres told them. 'If we cannot present our government with a viable military option, then we do not have the right to fly the flag of Zionism in Israel.'

General Gur agreed, but reiterated that any plan he presented to the cabinet must have a real chance of success. Furthermore, he stated, it must protect the hostages. Their lives must be the primary objective.

'Agreed,' said Peres. 'So where do we begin?'

They began by calling in a group of people who had worked in Uganda with Idi Amin. Many of these people had provided military training facilities for Ugandan forces when relations were good between the two countries. Others had taken part in the construction of Entebbe Airport and were able to provide drawings and plans of the old and new terminals. Others were from the intelligence community, which was already setting up links with contacts in Kampala.

Whilst this meeting was in progress, General Gur's deputy commanders began calling in a number of senior officers who would head the planning teams. Each team would concentrate on one possible military operation, provided it fulfilled the conditions laid down by General Gur and the Minister of Defence. These conditions were that the hostages must be placed at the smallest possible risk, that the strike force should reach Entebbe undetected, and that there should be a real chance of taking the airport and holding it until the hostages had been evacuated. Many of the officers who headed these teams were generals with considerable tactical experience.

In Shimon Peres's office the discussion turned to Idi Amin. One by one the people who knew him agreed that the Ugandan President would shelter the hijackers and ignore any pleas for assistance from Israel. Many went further than this. The President, they said, was a totally irrational and brutal dictator whose megalomania would result in one demand after another. Even if they agreed to the first ultimatum and released the prisoners, they believed there would be new conditions made, endless obstacles and, finally, demands so impossible that the hostages would be killed.

It was a bleak picture, but there were reasons to hope Amin would act cautiously. One of the people who knew him well believed that the President would never dare to be party to the deaths of such a large, multi-national group which included French, German, Americans and British in addition to the Israelis.

Whilst life in Uganda might be cheap, Amin had a healthy respect for the power and anger of Western governments. They agreed, therefore, that at this stage there was no immediate danger of the situation deteriorating. The President would almost certainly act as mediator. By flattering his ego this process could be protracted for some time.

Towards the end of the afternoon General Gur

and Defence Minister Peres went to Jerusalem and met the Crisis Cabinet appointed by Prime Minister Rabin to deal with the crisis. At 5.30 p.m. they met in the oak-panelled cabinet room beneath a large painting of Jerusalem and listened with grim faces to the General's assessment of the situation.

This inner group was composed of five ministers: Shimon Peres, Gad Yaakobi, Hein Zadok, Foreign Minister Yigal Allon and Prime Minister Rabin. It soon became obvious that whilst Shimon Peres and Gad Yaakobi, the Transport Minister, were looking for a military option, the remainder of the group were already thinking in terms of, at the most, a compromise with the terrorists.

The pressure was on General Gur who had to tell the cabinet, in all honesty, that at this time he had no military solution. He explained that, less than thirty hours after the hijack, he had insufficient data on the military strength of the Ugandans in Entebbe, the displacement of their forces and the number, condition, and location of the hostages.

Premier Rabin turned to his cabinet and said: 'These are the professionals. Are you ready to ignore their advice?'

Shimon Peres had been a political adversary of Yitzhak Rabin for many years. He had fought him in the election for the position of prime minister and had only narrowly been beaten. They were men of sharply contrasting temperaments and, although there was respect, there was little friendship between them. This was never more apparent than now when the Defence Minister bluntly demanded approval for some form of military action which he believed was necessary to counter the current image of a weak and indecisive government.

Rabin went crimson with anger. 'We are not talking about politics,' he said sharply. 'We are talking about a feasible military option which you do not have.'

The Defence Minister insisted that the army should go ahead with plans to counter the situation in Uganda, but Rabin did not want further discussions. He called for a vote and the Crisis Cabinet agreed that the government should continue to explore the possibility that negotiations with the Palestinians might gain the release of the hostages without bloodshed. But it also agreed, under pressure from Shimon Peres and Gad Yaakobi, that the army and intelligence community should continue to search for a viable military alternative.

That decision gave General Gur and his staff the time they needed. Teams of officers worked through the night, gathering information and

26

exploring every avenue that each new report opened. Intelligence had now confirmed that the hijackers had the full support of Ugandan ground troops at the airport and that the hostages were being held in the main lounge of the old terminal building, disused since the new terminal building had been constructed some years before by the Israeli firm of Solel Boneh. Reports on the strength of the Ugandan army units at Entebbe, which had originally placed the figure at almost a thousand, now reduced the total to about two hundred. But these forces could quickly draw on a large Ugandan Army camp only a few hundred yards from the perimeter of the airport which held between one thousand five hundred and two thousand soldiers together with a formidable armoury.

By Tuesday a number of plans were emerging from the military think tank, but in General Gur's opinion all of them had an element of risk so great as to swing the odds in favour of the Palestinians. The plans ranged from decoy aircraft to an air drop at night and assault by a Boeing 707, ostensibly carrying the released prisoners, but in fact crammed with Israeli commandos.

Throughout the many meetings that followed, General Gur and Defence Minister Peres reiterated that any raid must have the element of total surprise so that the terrorists had no time to turn on their hostages. This was the fear that haunted General Gur during the days that followed; that he might launch an attack which would lead to the deaths of the men, women and children they were trying to save. Such an attack, irrespective of the military outcome, would be a disastrous failure.

On Tuesday night, General Gur was not filled with optimism.

Chapter 4

The old terminal building at Entebbe was a long, two-storey structure which had fallen into decay in recent years. Inside was the main hall with a connecting door to a second, smaller hall. When the hostages arrived, this door had been sealed off with strips of wood nailed across it. The walls were cracked and dusty, lined with a few wooden benches. At night it was bitterly cold, by day stuffy and hot. For the hostages it was more cramped and uncomfortable than any prison cell.

For young Nadia Israel it was a bewildering world. Outside the building Ugandan soldiers patrolled or stood around in groups, their automatic rifles a constant menace. Inside there were usually one or two of the Palestinian hijackers, men who showed only angry contempt for the huddled mass of people. And there was the German woman, always striding arrogantly among them, swinging the pistol in her hand as

29

though she would love the chance to use it.

When they arrived in the terminal they had begun to realize that they were expected. An airport official had been there to welcome them with trays of sandwiches and cold drinks. The toilets and main hall had been cleared and made ready for use, and the airport official assured them that he had obtained plenty of food and they had nothing to worry about. His idea of plenty of food turned out to be rice, bananas, potatoes and poorly cooked meat. It never varied. And for many of the Jews who were Kosher the meat was unacceptable.

The first time they saw Idi Amin they had begun to feel that perhaps things would not be so bad. He had landed in a helicopter and moved jovially towards them with his four-year-old son. Both had been dressed in identical camouflage uniforms, and over Amin's left breast were Israeli paratrooper wings.

'For those of you who don't know me,' he began, and then broke into a laugh as if the very idea was impossibly funny. 'But I am sure all of you do know me and have heard of me. I am Field-Marshal Dr Idi Amin Dada, President of the Republic of Uganda.'

He had beamed at them, and then launched into a long speech explaining the rights of the Palestinian people and the reasons why they were being held as hostages. But having said this, he opened his arms, as though embracing them all.

'You must not worry,' he said. 'I will take care of you like a father. I will see that you are released.'

He grinned broadly and puffed out his chest, tapping himself with a fat finger. 'I am good to you.'

That first time, many of the hostages were convinced he was sincere and had applauded him enthusiastically at the end of his speech. They set about organizing themselves in the large hall, forming into groups of ten or twelve, telling each other that it would not be for long. A few hours, perhaps. A day at the most.

Sarah Davidson, with her husband Uzi and their two sons, Benji and Ron, had brought playing cards with them from the aircraft and they began playing bridge in one corner of the room. Nadia Israel and her aunt, Nina, joined the family, together with Pasco Cohen who had an infectious sense of humour and cheered everyone up by telling them gleefully that he was an expert in survival.

'You don't know how lucky you all are,' he told them. 'You are in the company of a specialist in getting out of tight places. I was one of the few survivors of the holocaust. I've taken part

31

in all of Israel's wars. I've faced death many times. I'm an expert in the business of staying alive.'

Sarah Davidson began to organize children into play groups, and in another part of the room Mrs Ruth Gross, a school teacher from Tel Aviv, set up a class for the young children, inventing numerous things for them to do. Mrs Gross was travelling with her husband, Baruch, and their six-year-old son, Shy, and became a focal point for many of the children.

Arika Lexer, a tall young lawyer from Tel Aviv, began to make himself known to the hijacker Boese, trying to draw him out about the aims of his group. Boese told him that he had been a great admirer of Ulrike Meinhof, the German anarchist leader, and that he believed she had been murdered by the German authorities.

Ulrike had been found hanged in her cell in Stuttgart the previous May whilst her trial was in progress, and both the inquest and the prison authorities had established that this was suicide. But Boese did not believe them. There had been reports of bruises on her legs and traces of semen on her clothes which would, if true, indicate that she had first been raped. Almost immediately after the news of her death he began training for the hijack operation.

Boese also told Arika Lexer that when he was operating with a Baader Meinhof cell in Germany he had been involved in the bombing of a supermarket in West Berlin. He did not appear to care about the consequences of the hijacking and admitted that he had expected to come out of it either dead, or with a long prison sentence. 'But not now,' he added. 'Not now we are here in Uganda.'

The captain and crew of the French airbus were a constant source of comfort and guidance for the people in the terminal. Throughout each day they were moving from group to group, helping, consoling, assisting with any chore. On many occasions members of the crew helped to clean the room, to supervise the distribution of food and organize activities.

Captain Bacos enjoyed a special respect from the Ugandans and the hijackers and used this skilfully to obtain concessions and information about developments in the negotiations. But in spite of the efforts of everyone to cope with the discomfort and spartan conditions, time dragged and each hour seemed like a day. By Tuesday spirits had begun to fall, people were beginning to doubt whether there would be any end to it. There had been two more visits from President Amin, resplendent in a different uniform on each occasion, and these had served to lift their spirits. He would tell them he was looking after them like a father.

'We are all children of God,' he proclaimed on one occasion. 'We love each other and I will see that no harm comes to you.'

But these words no longer rang as true as they had on Sunday. There were now at least ten Palestinian terrorists moving freely around the airport, and none of them seemed remotely disturbed by the hundred or so armed Ugandan soldiers who had the terminal building under constant guard.

And there was Bouvier, the suave leader of the terrorists. He was always immaculately dressed, chatting in the friendliest of terms with Ugandan officers and President Amin. He came and went in a white Mercedes driven by a Ugandan soldier, sometimes taking one or two of his men with him into Kampala.

The hostages were beginning to realize that the Ugandan president could, if he wished, take over the terminal and release them at any time. There were rumours that the airbus standing at the end of the runway had been mined, but there was no evidence of similar precautions in the terminal itself.

Michel Cojot, a French company executive who had been acting as a go-between with the passengers and the hijackers, had been convinced since Sunday that the situation was more serious than they had been led to believe.

He had seen Amin and the Palestinians chatting in a far too friendly way, and on more than one occasion had witnessed the open respect and affection towards the hijackers expressed by the Ugandan soldiers on duty at the terminal. Although the hijackers carried guns, there was never any suggestion that these were for protection against the Ugandans.

But the most telling memory for Cojot was the moment of arrival, when the soldiers had run towards the terrorists and embraced them, shouting and laughing. Their manner had been one of triumph, of congratulating comrades on a successful operation.

Tuesday was undoubtedly the worst of the days that were to follow. Nadia Israel was sitting with her aunt and the Davidson family, who were playing bridge, when Boese entered the room with two of the Palestinians and called for attention. His manner was smooth and pleasant, first congratulating them on the way they were coping with a situation which he knew was difficult, then assuring them that it would not last for much longer. Negotiations were going well, it was just a matter of time.

'The problem in here is that things are very crowded and this is obviously making life difficult for you all,' he said. 'We have decided that it will be best to put some of you in the next room.'

He pointed towards the door which was barricaded with strips of wood. 'From now on some of you will occupy that room.'

At first it seemed a good idea, but as the lists of names were produced, names drawn from the passports which had been seized on the plane, the awful truth began to dawn on the Jews. Every name that was called out was Israeli, or had a Jewish sound. People began to protest, others to cry. Fear swept through the room as the German woman and her Palestinian comrades stepped forward on either side of Boese, their expressions hard and watchful.

Nadia Israel was more frightened than she had ever been in her life. She had read books and heard the old people talk about how it was in the concentration camps and what it meant to be a Jew, but never had she ever imagined that this could one day happen to her.

With dry mouth and trembling hands she looked at the people around her. One old woman had begun to scream and shake, falling to her knees and flailing her arms as though to ward off the hijackers. The German woman gazed at her with contempt and gestured with her pistol towards the other room. The woman lost control completely, screaming and shaking so much that people caught hold of her and tried to stop her pulling at her hair.

Boese seemed concerned and slightly be-wildered by her behaviour, until he was told by Pasco Cohen and others that this woman had been in a Nazi concentration camp during the war. The segregation of Jews from Gentiles was an experience she would never forget, and now it was happening again: Germans with guns in their hands, segregating the Jews.

Boese flushed and told Cohen sharply that he was not a Nazi. He then asked them to tell the woman that she could remain with the other passengers in the first room.

'There is nothing sinister in this,' he assured them. 'It is simply that we have to put about a hundred of you in the other room, and as there are about that many Jews it is better that you be together.'

But the fear was still there. One by one they crossed to the door, crouching down and crawling under the nailed pieces of wood. Some cried as they went through. Children hung back, afraid, until their parents pulled them into the other room. The hijackers watched with stony faces, only Boese showing emotion.

Sarah Davidson, who had spoken to him once or twice, studied his face and found it troubled. It was as though he had only begun to realize the uncomfortable analogy with Nazi Germany, and with a shiver of fear she wondered if he knew more. Could this be the end for all the Jews in Entebbe?

The feeling grew for the remainder of the day and she found it difficult to sleep that night. In the early hours of the morning, when the children were asleep, she found Uzi awake and spoke to him about it. He laughed at her fears.

'There will be nothing like that,' he told her. 'In a day or two we will be back in Israel.'

The following day, as though to support this, 47 of the passengers in the large room were taken out and flown to Paris, and Ugandans arrived with lorry-loads of blankets and mattresses. Later that day President Amin came to see them, wearing the uniform of an admiral. Pointing proudly to the bedding, he told them that this was an example of how he was taking care of them all.

'Already we have sent some of your people home. Soon you will all go home. You see how I look after you.'

Sarah Davidson, like many of the hostages, believed him on Wednesday. Although her group had been given three mattresses, she had told her family not to use them as they looked as though they might be full of fleas. But this did not alter the fact that Idi Amin had provided them, in the same way as he was providing food.

Her spirits began to lift and looking around at the others in their room she saw people smiling and chatting again. The children had begun to play, running in and out of the groups, tumbling on mattresses as though they were a new and delightful luxury.

One group had made a draught-board on the floor and was absorbed in a game, using bottle tops as chequers. Others were reading or reminiscing about the past and Israel. Most of them were worried about their relatives and parents at home, how they might be feeling, but they tried to convince each other that the news in the papers would be full of optimism.

One woman in particular felt this. She was Mrs Nili Ben-Dor whose husband Hapoel was a football player for the Beersheba team. The proudest moment of his life had been when he was selected to play for Israel at the Olympic Games in Montreal, and he was in London at the moment completing his final training with the team. She was desperately hoping that something would happen soon, so that he could stop worrying and concentrate on playing well.

The hijackers and Ugandan guards had begun to let small groups of women and children go out of the terminal, walking around on the tarmac at the front of the building. Sarah Davidson welcomed a chance to get some fresh air. She walked briskly around the paved area, then stopped and looked across the airfield to the runway where the airbus shimmered in the sun.

It seemed a lifetime since she had boarded that aircraft with her husband and children for what was to have been the happiest journey of their lives.

Chapter 5

In Jerusalem the Israeli Prime Minister was facing a mountain of problems. To negotiate directly with the Palestinians was anathema to Israel, but to deal through a complex chain of diplomatic bureaux took endless hours, and at the end of each exchange the cabinet had to consider and frame a reply.

Messages were being sent by cable to the Israeli Embassy in Paris, from there to the French Foreign Service, which in turn passed them on to the Somali Ambassador. He passed the message to Idi Amin in Kampala, who passed it on to Bouvier, who then communicated with Waddie Haddad in Somalia on the contents of each cable and the answer they should give.

The delays and frustrations grew by the hour and opinion within the cabinet began to divide. One view was that direct negotiations should commence with the Palestinians, a move which would be seen as virtual capitulation by Israel. The other was that a military option was becoming increasingly vital, if only because Germany had already indicated that it was more than reluctant to consider releasing members of the Baader Meinhof group. With an election coming up, politicians knew that their careers were in the balance. The German public would find it very hard to forgive such a surrender to the terrorists.

One of the people sent to Paris at this time was Major-General Rehavam Zeevi, one of Israel's 'hawks' and a government adviser on methods of countering terrorist activity. One of his duties was to question hostages released by the hijackers and to pass the information back to Israel. At the same time Israeli intelligence agents were being flown to Kenya, from where they would infiltrate Uganda and make their way to Kampala.

By Wednesday the cabinet members were being told by Defence Minister Shimon Peres that a military option was now a real possibility due to the efforts of the planning teams. But Premier Rabin was adamant. Negotiations through proper diplomatic channels would continue. He did not feel that military action was in any way attractive, or warranted by the present situation.

Shimon Peres pointed out with exasperation that the deadline was running out. Rabin replied that there was every likelihood that the Palestinians would extend the deadline, and Peres was forced to agree.

In Tel Aviv General Gur was discussing that very possibility with Colonel Baruch (Borka) Bar-Lev. The colonel, a short, thickset man, was born in Lithuania and had once served with the British in the Jewish settlement police. He was now retired from the army, but had been head of the Israeli mission in Uganda when Idi Amin staged his coup in 1971. Since then, in spite of the hostility between the two countries, Bar-Lev had remained on good terms with the Ugandan President. Since the hijacking on Sunday he had been speaking to Amin at least once a day, doing his utmost to persuade him to act against the terrorists.

'Borka, my friend, you don't understand,' President Amin had told him. 'They have put dynamite on the plane, dynamite in the building. What can I do?'

'You take control, Idi. I cannot believe you do not have control of what is going on in Uganda. This is a chance given to you by God. Use it.'

'Borka,' Amin answered cheerfully. 'All you have to do is persuade your government to let the prisoners go. Give them the people they have asked for.'

'Idi, this is a marvellous chance for you,' Bar-Lev said. 'If you save the hostages you could get the Nobel Peace Prize.'

The colonel's report on the conversation was not optimistic. He was convinced that President Amin was playing games with them. Behind the guile, the frequent protestations of sympathy, was a ruthless and devious man intent on boosting his own prestige in Africa and establishing a strong position with the Palestinian movement.

Such a man, Bar-Lev suggested, would not be prepared to settle for anything less than the terms of the ultimatum. But, if anything, it was in his interests to drag the negotiations out as long as possible. This at least meant the present deadline was almost certain to be extended.

President Amin would resist any attempt to replace him as mediator, or to make arrangements for the exchange of hostages on neutral territory. Foreign Minister Allon was already endeavouring to achieve both these aims, and had appealed to the United Nations Secretary General, Kurt Waldheim, to intercede and take over the role of negotiator with the hijackers.

General Gur held a meeting with his deputy commanders and reviewed the plans drawn up so far. The large number of hostages had become a major factor in planning any rescue attempt. To evacuate close to two hundred people would require at least two aircraft in addition to the transport required for the attacking force. The optimum time on the ground was placed at only fifty minutes.

It was a formidable prospect, made worse by the fact that a surprise attack would only be possible with a small force. Any large concentration of aircraft would be detected hours before it reached Entebbe, giving the Ugandans time to organize their defences. These defences would include the squadrons of Mig 17s and 21s that were stationed at Entebbe, and the bulk of Amin's 20,000 strong army stationed in and around Kampala, only an hour's drive away.

General Peled and General Adam, however, both told their Chief-of-Staff that, in spite of the overwhelming odds, a successful mission was possible if they were able to hit Entebbe by surprise. Beni Peled outlined his proposed route, showing how the giant Hercules aircraft, the Lockheed C130Hs, would fly out of Israel's furthermost air base, Sharm el Sheik on the edge of the Red Sea. The aircraft would fly at no more than two hundred feet above the water, effectively below the radar screens operating in Egypt, Libya, the Sudan and Saudi Arabia. The C130s, Peled told them, would fly in tight formation, wing-tip to wing-tip, using sophisticated navigation equipment to maintain height and position. At the same time they would be joined by a Boeing 707, flying from Tel Aviv, which would be 20,000 feet above them for the crucial stage of the journey along the Red Sea.

The Boeing, Peled maintained, would show clearly on radar screens and would be assumed to be the scheduled flight from Tel Aviv to Nairobi. As the Boeing turned across Ethiopia for Kenya, the C130s would lift up from the sea and begin flying through the valleys of Ethiopia below. By hopping ridges, holding to the contours of the land, they could reach Kenya without detection. At that point they would turn again over Lake Victoria, and be on their final approach into Entebbe.

'It can be done,' said Peled. 'We can be two minutes from Entebbe before anyone knows we have left Israel.'

General Adam presented various options for the attack on Entebbe itself. They ranged from a paratroop drop over the old terminal, to simultaneous landings by the C130s. But General Gur was still not convinced that they had a feasible plan.

Shimon Peres returned from Jerusalem and General Gur joined him in his office.

'I have to tell you,' said the Chief-of-Staff, 'that in my view all the plans are defective in

46

some way. There are elements of recklessness which would jeopardize the safety of the hostages.'

They discussed the plans in detail, then General Gur leaned back in his seat and began to tick off the objectives which were essential to any military option.

They must be able to reach Entebbe without detection, and in Peled's view this meant they could use a maximum of three aircraft.

They must land in such a way that the attacking force could reach the old terminal before the hijackers had a chance to turn their guns on the hostages. They estimated no more than one minute could be allowed for this, after that the element of surprise would be lost.

They must simultaneously take the new terminal building, the control tower, and the road running from the airfield to the Ugandan Army camp a quarter of a mile down the road.

They must destroy the radar equipment and the Mig fighters to prevent pursuit in the air.

Finally, they must get the hostages in the air within fifty minutes of the first landing. After that time the Ugandan Army based at Kampala might be moving to the airport in strength and there would be a real chance that the C130s would not get off the ground.

This last possibility was the fear that dominated General Gur's thinking: to be so close to a rescue, only to find the hostages involved in a battle, or killed as their aircraft took off. Both Shimon Peres and General Gur agreed that this was a risk they could not take.

The two men knew, with a deep sense of frustration, that they could not fulfil the requirements of a successful operation. There would be too many hostages, too few planes. There was too little time, too great a risk. The only effective assault of Entebbe would have to be a massive one in which the Israelis overwhelmed the enemy on the ground and in the air. And this, they both knew, would never be approved by the cabinet.

Shimon Peres went to the window and stared grimly out at the grounds below. Soldiers came and went, the lights were beginning to come on in the city beyond. The roads were heavy with traffic, cars jostling each other in a way that only the Israeli motorist can do.

In Shimon Peres was a deep conviction that capitulation would escalate into something far worse. To hand over 53 key terrorists would give the Palestinians the strength and the incentive to seize more aircraft, make ever increasing demands. Even after the prisoners had been handed over he did not believe the hostages would be released. If that was the intention of the hijackers, they would surely have already agreed to the United Nations acting as mediator and to a neutral territory for the exchange.

And yet, to abandon some two hundred helpless people to their fate was equally unacceptable. He turned back to General Gur with taut features, finding his own emotions reflected in the face of his Chief-of-Staff.

'We must go on developing the most effective plan,' he said. 'There is a chance that the situation will change. Everyone agrees that Amin will not risk alienating major powers, and he has already released some of the hostages. If he were to release more . . . ?'

General Gur nodded. Of the remaining hostages at least a hundred were not Jews. If those were released they would be left with a number they could handle. Such a development would overcome many of the obstacles which at present seemed insurmountable.

It would be the hijackers biggest mistake and yet, if they did not intend to release the Jews in the end, it would be a mistake they would at some stage have to make.

Chapter 6

A grim and weary cabinet reached its decision in Jerusalem on Thursday. They would agree to release a number of the prisoners demanded by the Palestinians, but they first required certain guarantees that the hostages would be handed over unharmed.

Premier Rabin took the decision after a long and emotional meeting. Defence Minister Peres and Transport Minister Yaakobi were both pressing for a military option, but at the same time they agreed that such a move by the government would give them valuable time to take their planning further.

The decision was cabled to Paris and from there, via the Somali Ambassador, to Kampala. The reaction from the hijackers was swift. They would extend the deadline until noon on Sunday, and as a gesture were releasing a further 101 hostages who would be flown to Paris immediately.

There was relief and renewed hope among the ministers at the news, but it was short-lived. When the hostages arrived in Paris there was not a Jew among them. Every single hostage remaining in Entebbe was of Jewish origin.

Shimon Peres called an immediate meeting in his office at the Ministry of Defence in Tel Aviv.

'Now we know,' he told his generals. 'Now we know the game they play.'

The hundred or so hostages in Entebbe were the real pawns in the game, the ones who would be expended with ruthless determination. Peres declared grimly that whatever action they took should be taken before Sunday. They had just forty-eight hours to plan and execute the rescue operation. A full staff meeting was called in which General Gur brought in the men who would lead and command the attack on Entebbe. The plan he presented to them would now work because of the reduced number of hostages. It was their job to turn it into a practical reality.

The man chosen to command the force was Israel's senior operational soldier, Brigadier Dan Shomron. Dan Shomron was a solidly built man, aged 39, who had established a reputation in the IDF as a soldier of courage and great ingenuity. His hair was black, slightly curly, his mouth relaxed and given to smiling. In spite of his rank of brigadier, he adopted a casual and friendly manner with all his men and, over the years, had built up the kind of loyalty that was invaluable in battle.

He joined the paratroops in 1955 and took part in the retaliatory raids of that period, and in the Sinai campaign. During the Six Day War he had commanded the battalion which was the first to reach the northern end of the Suez Canal, an achievement he quickly attributed to the bravery and enthusiasm of his men. For that accomplishment he was awarded the Exemplary Conduct Medal.

Following the Six Day War, Shomron fought against terrorists in the Jordan Valley, carrying out many hazardous swoops on terrorist camps. During the War of Attrition he again adopted this commando-style role, making lightning attacks into Egypt to destroy supplies and communications.

Shomron then began training in Israel's armoured division to become a tank officer. The military chiefs recognized his considerable abilities and his liking for fast, precision raids which always succeeded in catching the enemy on the wrong foot. He was a born leader and during the Yom Kippur War he commanded the armoured brigade, once again showing his brilliance by completing the encirclement of the Third Army and effectively reversing the tide of battle

There had been no doubt in General Gur's mind that the natural choice to carry a lightning strike against Entebbe was Brigadier Shomron.

For Shomron it was the most important command of his career. As Chief Paratroop and Infantry Officer in the Israeli Defence Force he was able quickly to draw up a list of key men who would head the various units in the attack force. At no time did he have the slightest doubt that, once on the ground at Entebbe, they could reach the hostages and overwhelm the opposition. The problem was getting on the ground without alerting the Ugandan Army.

Together with Beni Peled and Yekuti Adam he worked through the night, perfecting a plan which was so audacious that everyone concerned was infected by the excitement.

The essence was speed and mobility on the ground, using a lightly equipped main force to take the old terminal before anyone realized that an attack was under way. Previous plans had made use of the main runway, striking at the control tower and new terminal building before encircling the old buildings – or in one case dropping paratroopers on that area.

Shomron proposed to land a giant Lockheed C130H transport aircraft on the old runway which passed half a mile from the building where the hostages were kept. Because of the very short landing distance required by these aircraft, Shomron believed it would be possible to land, turn off the runway and taxi almost up to the terminal itself, giving his men the enormous advantage of surprise.

The transport of the units from Israel was the responsibility of the air force. It was clear that the base from which they would operate must be Sharm el-Sheikh. It was also obvious that the smaller the force, the better their chances of reaching Entebbe undetected.

Shomron recommended a force of 180 men, supported by armour-plated jeeps with fixed machine-guns. These could be carried by the large Hercules aircraft, which had rear cargo doors that dropped down to form a ramp. The men would be lightly equipped with Uzi sub-machine-guns, machine-pistols and the new Galil assault rifle and grenades, enabling them to run fast for the terminal.

His primary targets at the airport were the control tower and its radar room, the new terminal building where Ugandan soldiers would be on duty, the old tower which they knew was being used by Ugandan soldiers guarding the hostages, and the squadrons of Mig 21s and Mig 17s which were parked at the airport. Small units would attack each of these targets whilst the main force went for the hostages.

A major obstacle to taking and holding the airport was the existence of the Ugandan Army camp several hundred yards from the perimeter. Intelligence sources reported that there were almost two thousand soldiers in this camp, with a wide range of arms and equipment. Shomron proposed that a paratroop unit should set up road blocks and an ambush on the road to the camp, with the object of fighting a delaying action there for as long as possible.

There were still elements in the plan which General Gur regarded as risky, but it had all the requirements he and Defence Minister Peres had laid down. At this stage it was a feasible option.

The question of air cover to protect the transport aircraft from Egyptian and Libyan fighters was of paramount importance, but the Israeli Mirage and Phantom fighters did not have the range to escort the task force beyond the Red Sea. To refuel the fighters over the Red Sea would involve the use of brilliant lights on the tanker aircraft, together with extensive radio transmissions which would almost certainly be picked up by Saudi Arabia. It was finally agreed that fighter cover should be provided to the limit of the possible range, and that the Hercules would then continue on their own. By this time they would be close to Ethiopia and preparing to cut across that country towards Kenya.

Fortunately the C130s were equipped with American radar jamming devices and these could well convince long-range radar operators that atmospheric conditions were causing trouble with their equipment. Another vital asset was the sophisticated navigational equipment in the Hercules. This equipment would enable them to fly blind for 2000 miles without any help from air traffic controllers.

The excitement grew as step by step the final plan emerged. The logistics of what they were planning were enormously complex. To support such a tactical force on the ground in a hostile country meant that the command post, manned by Peled and Adam, could be in only one place: thirty thousand feet above Entebbe for the duration of the operation.

'I can operate over Entebbe,' Peled told them. 'I can get your people in and out, and hold station above until they're clear of the airfield.'

Even as the final planning conference was in progress, an American hostage who had been released and flown to Paris, was arriving in Tel Aviv to provide an eye-witness account of the Ugandan strength at the airport, the location of the hostages and the routine being followed by the hijackers.

He spent many hours with Intelligence officers and then spoke to the generals planning the operation. His information, together with valuable data being passed to Tel Aviv from a diplomatic source in Kampala, put the final pieces into place. The planners knew where the hostages were being held, how, and that no more than one hundred and twenty Ugandan soldiers were guarding the terminal.

But what interested the generals most of all were the regular visits by Idi Amin. It was these which were to provide the most crucial element of the plan, for everyone agreed that unless they could be in action around the terminal within one minute of landing the lives of the hostages would be in great danger.

Even though the upper floors of the military headquarters in the Kiryah were a hive of activity, the ministers and generals had to appear natural and to go about their normal lives. General Gur's father-in-law had died the previous day and his body was being flown to Israel. At the height of the planning session the General had to go to Ben Gurion Airport and receive the coffin, for if he had not done so people would have begun to talk. Secrecy was vital, so ministers continued to go to parties. Generals attended receptions in which people consoled them for their inability to act and the sad surrender of the government to the terrorist demands.

They were not to know that army headquarters was a powerhouse of energy that night: hand-picked personnel were being drawn in from units all over Israel. Paratroopers, members of the Golani mountain troops, men from Israel's elite commando units. Many of them were senior officers in command of units, but on this occasion it did not matter. In some ways, this was to be the night of the generals.

Beni Peled was briefing his own staff on the transportation problems they must solve before Saturday. Together with his air commanders he finalized the route they would follow from Sharm el-Sheikh down the Red Sea. Fighter cover, by Mirages and Phantoms, would be provided for the first 1000 miles at their maximum height of 60,000 feet. Far below, skimming the waves, would be three C130s in tight formation, moving as one.

When the fighters turned back towards Israel the Boeing 707, flying along a slightly different route from Tel Aviv, would move into position above the giant Hercules transport aircraft for the crucial leg past the border of Saudi Arabia before they turned inland over Ethiopia. The presence of the Boeing, which would be taken to

Tactical approach map

be the scheduled flight to Nairobi, would lessen the chances of the radar operators detecting any trace of activity at sea level. Even if the screens did show something, the chances were that the operators would assume it was a reflection from the Boeing caused by atmospheric conditions.

The Boeing 707, Peled told his commanders, would be equipped as a mobile hospital carrying ten doctors and operating personnel. It would land at Nairobi and remain there in the event of it being necessary to bring wounded from Entebbe. Some of his commanders suggested extending the range of the fighters by having a refuelling tanker cruising over Sinai, ready to move towards the returning fighters. This was ruled out because of the interest such an aircraft would create in Egypt and Libya. They might begin to wonder why, and then start to make guesses.

The refuelling of the C130s was a major headache. The aircraft would be carrying refuelling equipment which could be used at Entebbe if time and circumstances made it possible. If there was insufficient time the Hercules would have to carry on with what little fuel they had to a safe haven where they could refuel.

Kenya was an obvious choice for such a haven, as was Addis Ababa in Ethiopia. But the general view was that the Seychelle Islands presented the safest place for the attacking force. Providing the C130s had sufficient fuel when they took off from Entebbe, they would cross Kenya and fly out over the Indian Ocean to land at the main Seychelle Island of Mahe. The Boeing 707 from Nairobi would take off and fly with them. This would remove the danger of pursuit or attack from fighter aircraft going to Uganda's assistance. But it would stretch their fuel reserve to the limit. It was a strategy which depended on the weather conditions during the flight to Entebbe and the amount of fuel remaining in the tanks of the Hercules when they landed. It was one of the unknown factors, a decision which could only be taken at that phase of the operation.

The aerial command post presented a far more complex problem. The sophisticated communications equipment it would need, able to transmit back to Tel Aviv on a high frequency wavelength, meant General Peled had to use either one of the Air Force Boeing 707s, or a Hercules. There was no doubt that the Hercules had more space to provide a comprehensive operations room, but the Boeing would have the speed and manoeuvrability to get out of trouble. In the end it was the Boeing that was chosen.

One of the squadron commanders pointed out that if the Ugandans managed to get the Mig 17s and 21s off the ground the command plane would be a sitting target. Peled brushed the argument aside.

'Shomron's guys will take care of those,' he said.

It might be a daring plan, even a desperate gamble, but the military option which Shimon Peres and General Gur had asked for only two days before now existed.

In the office of the Minister of Defence, Shimon Peres was reading and rereading a letter he had received that day. It was from a twelve-year-old boy in Israel who had written to the minister to ask if the army could not go in and rescue the hostages in Entebbe.

The boy had thought very hard about the problem and had come up with a plan which he was suggesting to the Minister of Defence in the hope that somehow the IDF could carry it out.

The plan described in the letter was almost exactly the plan they had adopted.

Chapter 7

The men began to arrive on Friday morning. They came out of the desert, in helicopters and trucks and Hercules from Tel Aviv. They were lean young men with a laconic manner and an air of purpose about them. Many of them were oriental Jews, wiry and tough.

They were hand-picked, volunteers from the elite units of the IDF. Men from the armoured division, the paratroop regiment, the Golani infantry and the special tactical units operating around the Golan Heights and Sinai.

They moved into the air base at Sharm el-Sheikh on the edge of Sinai looking out over the Red Sea, and then they listened quietly as the briefing began.

The man Shomron had elected to lead the assault force which would take the old terminal building and rescue the hostages was Lieut.-Colonel Yonatan Netanyahu, one of the country's most outstanding young officers and commander of one of the elite units based in the Golan mountains.

Lieut.-Colonel Yoni Netanyahu was 30 years old and had been born in New York where his father had been on a mission for the Revisionist Movement. The family returned to the new-born state of Israel in 1948 and Yoni grew up in Jerusalem where he studied at the Gymnasia and became a leader in the scout movement.

In the Six Day War he distinguished himself in a number of actions but on the final day, during the attack on the Golan Heights, he was wounded. That autumn he left Israel and enrolled at Harvard University where he studied physics and philosophy, but after a year he returned and continued his studies at the Hebrew University.

When the War of Attrition began he decided to join the regular army and participated in many daring operations which quickly established him as an officer of courage and initiative. During the Yom Kippur war he commanded a unit on the Golan Heights which was involved in fierce battles with Syrian commandos. He was decorated for rescuing a wounded officer near the Syrian lines after a previous attempt had failed.

He was a man of medium height and build with black, curly hair and a ready grin. He had a dry sense of humour and a warm personality that extended to everyone he met. His qualities of leadership were exceptional, for he had that rare ability to project his own enthusiasm and vitality into those around him.

On Friday, 2 July, he worked his men remorselessly under the hot Sinai sun. Again and again they crowded into the fuselage of the C130, checked weapons and took positions, then looked towards Yoni.

'Go!' he would shout, starting the watch.

From the hold of the Hercules two jeeps roared down the ramp, followed by 50 men running hard with Uzi sub-machine-guns and Galil automatic assault rifles. They had to run 500 yards to an area marked out in the sand to the precise dimensions of the old terminal at Entebbe. The jeeps went straight for the front of the building, turning left and right so that they could cover the approaches to the building.

Behind them the men were fanning out, running for the side entrances and the rear. When every man was in position a whistle blew and Yoni checked his stop watch.

'Not good enough. Fifty-three seconds to clear the aircraft. It has to be forty-five.'

The run to the terminal had to be fast, each man moving by instinct to his respective positions. There would be no time to wait, to check if others were ready. Once they were into the doors and corridors of the terminal they went in. Shooting.

'Not fast enough,' said Yoni. 'I want you round the building and in action one and a half minutes after we touch the ground.'

And there were other exercises to rehearse.

They put 100 volunteer hostages on the sand and practised moving them out through the doors to the aircraft. The volunteers pretended to be wounded, afraid, sick. Yoni's men had to help, to lift them into the aircraft, carry them up the ramp. All the time the stop watch was ticking.

They sat in the shade as the commander went over the plan again and again. By the time the sun had begun to set they were coming out of the Hercules and fanning into position in 45 seconds. They were taking the terminal from every angle, into the main hall in ten minutes. They had the hostages out and on board the Hercules, with covering fire and units in control of the old control tower in a further twenty minutes. They worked with the ground crew who would be preparing to refuel the Hercules, learning what must be done.

Engineers who had built Entebbe Airport were on hand to brief them on the exact location of the valves and the underground tanks of fuel. The information the force was able to obtain from these engineers on various aspects of the buildings and installations at Entebbe could well have meant the difference between success and failure. As one soldier put it: 'The best thing Idi Amin did for Israel was to let them build his airport.'

When Lieut.-Colonel Netanyahu reported to Brigadier Shomron on Friday night he was confident and smiling. They would be ready for take-off within 45 minutes after landing, he told him.

Shomron's other commanders had also been hard at work. One force had rehearsed the positions they would move into to take the new terminal building. Another had been practising with a dummy control tower, running up flights of stairs, entering and destroying the radar equipment. Jeep drivers had rehearsed coming out of the C130 the moment its ramp was down, studying the layout of the Entebbe field so that they knew precisely how far to go and in which direction. Members of the demolition unit had worked on the explosive packs they would carry and planned where they would place them to destroy the Mig fighters on the ground.

There was also a special group, ten men who were part of Yoni's unit. They had been practising what was to be a critically important element of the operation; studying photographs, talking to a make-up specialist, choosing the unusual clothes they would wear. These men laughed a great deal. Particularly one very large Israeli who, in spite of his broad chest, was still stuffing padding into his camouflaged battle suit.

During Friday one of the C130s took off with General Gur and General Peled on board. For two hours it flew low over the sea, twisting and turning, whilst the Israeli radar stations tried to detect it.

On board General Gur presented Beni Peled with a variety of problems. They flew over flat, featureless desert to arrive at precise positions a hundred miles apart. They flew over water, over cloud, navigating blind with the sophisticated equipment on board.

When General Gur left his Commander of the Air Force, he was satisfied that tactically the aircraft and crews could carry out their part. But the day was only beginning for Beni Peled. With his air commanders he took off in three C130s and began flying in tight formation, working out the positions each pilot would take.

It was dangerous work, even in daylight. When the operation took place the most difficult part of their journey would be made at night.

At first the crews kept in touch by radio, checking each other's position, edging forward as they thundered through the sky at their maximum speed of 357 mph. Then Peled imposed radio silence, taking the lead aircraft himself and watching critically at each turn as the other aircraft followed.

They flew almost at zero feet, and then at 10,000, checking fuel consumption and the performance of the four large Allison turboprops which each developed 4,500 horse power. They also checked opening and closing cargo doors in flight, lowering the ramp so that it would be possible to jettison vehicles. They were all aware of the possibility that one or more of the C130s would be shot up on the ground at Entebbe, and this would mean crowding additional men into the remaining aircraft.

The day wore on. There were not enough hours. As darkness fell the Air Commander debated a night manoeuvre to check the system of code lights they had worked out, but his men had been flying all day, and the next night it would be for real.

They spent a further hour on the charts, a navigation expert going over the route they would take across Ethiopia. There would be moonlight, but not as much as they would have liked, for they would be ridge-hopping, dropping into valleys and following rivers. This way it would be impossible for radar stations to pick them up, to wonder why three strange transport aircraft were heading secretly towards Uganda.

Every man at Sharm el-Sheikh was aware of what it would mean if Idi Amin was waiting for them. He had close to 20,000 troops to put into Entebbe, although the Migs would make their presence unnecessary if they got into the air before the C130s touched down. But these risks had been weighed against the evidence that no one, least of all Uganda, could imagine that an Israeli task force would strike 2,000 miles from home with a mere handful of men.

Shomron was discussing the final points of the operation with General Adam. In front of them was a model of Entebbe Airport. Present also were members of the tactical planning team and Mossad, the Israeli Intelligence Service.

'We need insurance', Adam had said days before. 'We need men on the ground before we get there.'

At this briefing they learned who those men were to be, Israeli agents who had been flown to Kenya the moment the operation became a possibility and who had driven in cars, or concealed in battered African trucks, across the border and into Uganda. As early as Thursday some of these agents had been reconnoitring Entebbe airfield, radioing back information from transmitters deep in the bush, or in one case using the diplomatic facilities of an embassy.

On the night of the operation these men would

occupy two positions. One group would be in the new terminal building, ready to destroy the telephone cables connecting the airport with the outside world. The other was to take up position on the road between the Ugandan Army and the airfield, setting explosives so that vehicles or large bodies of men could be ambushed. These agents would be joined by a small detachment of Israelis from the landing force.

There would be other agents in Kampala, ready to alert the aerial command post the moment there were signs that the main Ugandan Army was getting ready to rush to the airport.

It was in this area that Beni Peled's aerial operations room provided its biggest bonus. At a height of 30,000 feet he could receive messages from handsets on the ground over a wide area. That area could comfortably take in the entire airfield, the surrounding camps and villages, and also the city of Kampala. As long as they could surprise Amin, there was little likelihood that he could surprise them.

Another major activity at the air base on Friday was preparation for the medical units on each aircraft. Thirty-three doctors had been selected, many of them from the Beth Sheba Medical Centre in Tel Aviv. They were all highly experienced surgeons, but their environment was the aseptic and organized world of the hospital operating theatre. On this mission, the details of which were not revealed to the majority of the doctors until the last briefing, they would mostly be operating in the cramped fuselages of C130s, either on the ground or in the air.

Ten of these doctors were assigned to the Boeing 707 at Tel Aviv. This they equipped with mobile operating theatres, the necessary drugs and instruments, together with 200 pints of plasma and a blood bank which had been checked against the blood types of every man on the operation. Wherever possible the blood types of the hostages had also been checked, but this aspect had to be played down for any open interest could break the vital wall of secrecy around the operation.

There had been reports from Kampala that day suggesting that the hostages were suffering from severe diarrhoea, so the senior medical consultant included in his supplies milk and medicines which could be administered on the flight from Entebbe.

In one of the briefing rooms the assault commanders were grouped around the model of the airport. Present at this briefing were men who had assisted in the construction of the Ugandan Airport. They were able to describe in detail the location of key rooms relating to communications, radar and power inputs. They answered questions for well over an hour so that by the time the commanders retired for the night, they knew the buildings intimately. They were supremely confident that they could take and hold Entebbe.

But at the Military Headquarters in Tel Aviv there was no such confidence. General Gur had deliberately encouraged his staff to pick every hole they could in the plans for the operation. Late on Friday night they were still finding obstacles, presenting possible situations which would turn the tide against them.

The weather forecast was already predicting turbulence over the Red Sea, and this could seriously jeopardize the ability of the C130s to skim the waves below the radar screen. At the best, it would leave them dangerously short of fuel when they reached Entebbe.

With this in mind they projected a bad weather pattern over the first 1,000 miles of the route, analysing the additional fuel and the height limitations such weather would impose. The results were disturbing. It could mean that, if it was not possible to refuel at Entebbe, there would be no chance of reaching the Seychelles. The need to use Kenya as a refuelling base was becoming more and more evident.

General Gur and his Second-in-Command, General Adam, discussed the situation with

73

Shimon Peres. The estimate of casualties was high; even if they caught the Ugandans totally off balance they would still have to contend with 120 Ugandan soldiers and the hijackers in the immediate vicinity of the terminal.

Colonel Netanyahu's force was highly trained in this kind of lightning raid, but on this occasion they would be forced to take every conceivable risk in order to reach the hostages before the hijackers could turn on them. This was the flaw. There would be no time to operate defensively on the ground, to move in with caution. From the moment the force left the aircraft they had to move as one for the terminal and take whatever risks were necessary until they had eliminated the terrorists.

General Gur had accepted the possibility of heavy casualties once the plan had been finalized, but he was adamant about medical facilities for his men. 'If it is necessary to use Nairobi, then we will use it. And if there is no other way, then we will use it by force.'

With grim features they discussed how this could be done. It meant a separate force at Nairobi, available if the Kenyan government, or the airport authorities, refused landing facilities to the C130s. The possible consequences of this action were not lost on the Generals or Shimon Peres, but with the weather situation deteriorating hourly over the Red Sea, the chances of reaching a country which would have no reason to turn them away, was becoming increasingly remote.

'Refuelling at Entebbe would be the complete answer,' one of the Generals pointed out. 'I suggest that we take additional ground crew, or put more emphasis on taking and holding the fuel valves at the airport.'

General Adam was reluctant to change the emphasis. He pointed out that the new terminal building and the control tower had to be taken and put out of action, just as the Mig fighters had to be destroyed. If the C130s were pursued by fighters with radar assistance they would easily be caught, and without fighter protection they would be quickly destroyed.

Additional aircraft were suggested, but everyone knew that three was the greatest number that could operate with any chance of secrecy. Beyond that the odds escalated, increasing the chances of the force being wiped out en route.

Shimon Peres discussed the question of Kenya with Foreign Minister Allon. His opinion was that, faced with aircraft in distress requesting medical aid and facilities, the Kenyans would accept them. But he also agreed that the presence of Israelis on the ground would be a guarantee the planners could not afford to ignore.

The Foreign Minister said, not without sadness, that they must use Nairobi and hope that the Kenyans did not become embroiled in Israel's struggle.

When Shimon Peres had his final meeting with General Gur and his staff they were still discussing the options open to them. The Generals were being deliberately obstructive, believing this was the only way they could envisage every contingency. It finally came down to the question: 'If we cannot be sure of Kenya, and cannot reach a friendly country, what then?'

General Gur's answer was simple and direct. 'We still go.'

When the meeting broke up there were many worried faces. They were playing with shadows, guessing at events which could change drastically one way or the other. The actual planning of the operation, which at first had seemed to be their most difficult task, was proving to be the least of their worries. The force was equipped and ready to move, and no one doubted its ability to carry out the operation as planned. It was the sequel to Entebbe that could become their biggest problem and turn victory into defeat.

The Chief-of-Staff knew all too well that once the action began in Uganda, the neighbouring country of Kenya would know. With relations badly strained between the two countries, and

Amin regularly making aggressive noises, their radar stations would be keeping a careful watch on Entebbe. They would have the complete picture long before the C130s left Uganda.

Before Shimon Peres left, General Gur asked him how sure he was of getting cabinet approval for the operation. The Prime Minister was still refusing to accept military intervention, but was under increasing pressure from other members of the cabinet and some of Israel's elder statesmen, including Golda Meir. 'If you do not have the courage to act,' the former Prime Minister had said, 'you will not be fit to walk with the dogs in the street.'

The Minister of Defence gave General Gur a bleak smile. 'It will be approved,' he said. 'After all, when they hear the impossible thing we intend to do, how can they refuse!'

That evening Shimon Peres had a guest for dinner. His name was Zbigniew K. Brzezinski, the chief adviser in foreign affairs for presidential candidate Jimmy Carter. He had arrived that day for unofficial talks with members of the government, a visit which the Israeli cabinet took very seriously as it was rumoured that this man could well replace Henry Kissinger if Carter became president.

It was unfortunate that his arrival should co-incide with Operation Entebbe. For most of the day the Minister of Defence had debated the wisdom of a meeting with a man already regarded as a shrewd and formidable observor. To postpone the meeting, however, would have led the American to the inevitable assumption that 'something was up'.

In the afternoon Brzezinski met with Premier Rabin and in the evening was delivered to the fifth floor apartment of Defence Minister Peres. The Head of Israeli Intelligence, Shlomo Gazit, had also been invited and Mrs Peres had prepared the meal herself in the modest living-room of the Peres apartment. For an hour they ate fish, chicken broiled in honey, salad and fresh fruit, and talked generally of the political and economic climate in the world.

Throughout the meal both Peres and his chief of intelligence knew that sooner or later the conversation would turn to Uganda. But they were quite unprepared for the direct, and shrewd, question that Brzezinski put to them.

'You know what I can't understand?' He said, looking genuinely puzzled. 'I can't make out why you guys don't go right into Uganda and take your people out? I mean, it seems to me the cleanest solution to a pretty lousy business.'

For almost a minute neither Shimon Peres or Shlomo Gazit dared to look at each other. Finally, with a completely expressionless face, the Minister of Defence acknowledged that 'it was a good idea'. He then spent an hour trying to prove to the American that such an operation was an impossible dream far beyond the resources and strategic limits of the IDF.

Throughout the discussion Zbigniew Brzezinski observed them with a shrewd and disturbingly intent manner. He offered alternatives, considered their negative assessments, but finally accepted with polite approval that the Israelis were in the best position to assess the situation and would act accordingly.

It was the most difficult meeting of the week for Shimon Peres and Intelligence Chief Shlomo Gazit, and when the American finally said goodnight they both had an uncomfortable feeling that his conclusion that they 'would act accordingly' had been deliberately phrased to encompass another possibility.

There was little sleep for Shlomo Gazit that night. As the weather continued to deteriorate over the Red Sea it became clear that Kenya was now the only option open to the task force. Messages went out to Israeli agents in Nairobi and during the early hours of Saturday morning they began to move into the airport, taking up key positions under the guise of maintenance workers, passengers in transit, even ground crew at the refuelling terminals. They were supported by a team of agents who had arrived two days earlier on board flight LY 535. These men, wearing El Al uniforms, were listed as relief crews for inbound flights due the following week. Every one of them was an Israeli secret agent.

Chapter 8

On Friday morning President Idi Amin presented himself at the terminal, accompanied by his attractive wife and his young son, Gamal abd al-Nazzar Ja-Wami. The President wore a suit and a wide-brimmed hat and greeted the hostages with '*Shalom*'. He told them that he was on his way to Mauritius where he would be discussing their problem at the meeting of the Organization for African Unity. His manner was grave and the hostages listened in tense silence as he berated their government for their failure to co-operate with the Palestinians.

'It is very serious,' he told them. 'I am doing everything I can for you, but if your own government will not also do everything there could be some bad trouble here. I do not want trouble. I want to be a father to you. You are all my children and as you have seen I am good to you. I do everything for you.'

There was silence in the room. In many faces

there was fear and apprehension. Amin went on to tell them that the terminal building was packed with explosives and that the terrorists would blow it up if their demands were not met. Boese, Tiedemann and three Arabs watched in silence, their faces betraying no emotion as Amin gestured towards them. Around Amin were his personal Palestinian guards. Outside, patrolling the tarmac in front of the terminal, were dozens of Ugandan soldiers with automatic rifles.

Pasco Cohen, sitting with a group which included Mr and Mrs Lipsky and a young man of nineteen called Jean Jacques Maimoni, voiced the question in many people's minds. If things were that serious, why did Amin not turn his weapons on the terrorists?

Amin looked at the hostages with grim features. 'You must also help,' he said. 'I advise you to write a letter to your government which I can have published on the radio and in the press. In it you must tell your government to agree to the demands. I tell you this sincerely. If you do not it will be bad here. I will not be able to help you.'

Again he reiterated the danger they faced. 'Your lives are in danger here,' he said, 'because of the obstinacy of your government.'

After the President had left for Mauritius a fierce argument broke out among the hostages.

Many of them, including most of the crew of the French airbus, were in favour of writing the letter. Others were opposed, particularly Captain Bacos who felt that they should hold out against the terrorists.

Captain Bacos and his crew were held in high regard by all the hostages. The previous day, when the terrorists had released 101 passengers, they had clearly wanted the crew also to return to France. The Captain had been adamant, however, declaring that none of his crew would leave Entebbe until the last hostage had been released.

The view of Captain Bacos, who had remained calm and authoritative throughout the week, was that to write such a letter would be tantamount to co-operating with the terrorists. He also believed that it would achieve nothing and would only serve to complicate the negotiations already in progress. Pasco Cohen was equally vociferous in his argument against it, saying that such a plea from the hostages would be publicized all over the world and would place pressure on the Israeli Government.

'We don't know what they are planning,' he said. 'We know nothing of what is happening in the outside world.'

Some of the hostages expressed cynicism at this view. 'What can they do?' One of them asked. 'They are two thousand miles away.' Others, such as Sarah Davidson, retained the hope that something would happen to break the deadlock. Although it had now been five days, she still believed that a solution would be found.

Captain Bacos finally bowed to the view of the majority and helped them to draft a letter which satisfied everyone. It also satisfied President Amin when he received it, and none of the hijackers appreciated the ambiguity in the words the hostages had chosen.

After thanking the terrorists for the good treatment they had received, the letter 'Urged the Israeli Government to *act* for the release of the hostages'. For many the use of the word 'act' could also suggest action, but few people on Friday really believed that a military option was possible.

A mood of depression had begun to grip many of the hostages, enhanced by the fierce argument that had raged over the letter. For many days they had been led to believe, both by the terrorists and by Amin, that their incarceration would be short-lived and that negotiations were going well. They now knew this was not the case, and around the room groups sat in miserable silence.

Many of them were recalling the ugly scenes of the previous day when the Arabs had taken four of the hostages into one of the side rooms and interrogated them for almost an hour. One of the men had been brutally beaten and a woman threatened.

With only Israelis remaining in the terminal, it seemed as though the hijackers were beginning to show a sadistic disregard for the feelings of their prisoners. The Arabs known as 39 and 55 found a game which amused them. With menacing expressions they marched into the centre of the room, holding up a list and telling the hostages to raise a hand when their name was called.

The Arab, 55, then called out a name while his companion glared and gestured with his gun until the person named raised a hand. The Arabs considered the person for a minute or so, then exchanged mysterious looks before making a mark beside the name. This went on for almost an hour until the Arabs grew tired of the game and went away.

The menacing attitude of the hijackers, together with the interrogation of some of the hostages, led to rumours of torture by electric shocks and threats of murder. There were scenes of near-hysteria as people succumbed to the fear that had been growing in them since Tuesday.

There was also sickness. Many of the people had begun to suffer from diarrhoea and, although the Ugandan doctor had been informed, nothing had so far been done. The drinking water was also deteriorating, becoming a dark brown colour, and it seemed in danger of running out altogether.

Outside the building some of the Ugandans had strung up a number of clothes lines and many of the women did what washing they could and hung clothes out to dry. Children were allowed to play in this area, and these were perhaps the least concerned of the hostages.

When the food arrived at noon on Friday it was the inevitable diet of rice, bananas and trays of badly-cooked stew. Shortly after they had begun to eat one of the women, Mrs Dora Bloch, swallowed a large piece of meat which became lodged in her throat. People around her became concerned and tried to help, but after a few minutes it became obvious that her condition was serious. One of the terrorists sent for the Ugandan doctor.

Mrs Dora Bloch was 73 years old and had been used as an interpreter on occasions because of her knowledge of languages. She was fluent in seven languages and could translate freely into Hebrew and French for many of the passengers who were unable to speak English. She was a calm, pleasant, grey-haired woman who was flying to New York with her son, Ilan Hartuv, for the wedding of her other son, Daniel.

When the Ugandan doctor arrived she was having great difficulty in breathing and was in considerable distress. Ilan begged the doctor to do something, but after trying to free the piece of lodged meat he said she would have to be taken to hospital. Friends comforted the elderly woman until an ambulance arrived, and then she was taken to the hospital in Kampala.

The incident seemed to depress people further and as the day wore on there were more cases of sickness and diarrhoea. The toilets, barely adequate to begin with, became blocked and the effect was distressing on people already suffering from nausea and sickness. To add to their discomfort the water in the washroom finally ran out. People began to lose the control that they had somehow maintained throughout the week.

Sarah Davidson continued to play cards with her two sons, using the game to take their minds off the situation around them. She played on their determination to beat her, forcing them to concentrate so that they never got a chance to grow bored. Her husband, Uzi, had been absorbed in a book for two days now and although his calmness and strength was a great comfort, she was getting exasperated with him. Finally she asked him what on earth it was that kept him buried in a book all the time. Uzi told her that he was reading a novel called *The Eagle Has Landed*, by a British writer named Jack Higgins.

'It's all about a commando raid on an isolated part of England to kidnap Winston Churchill and hold him as hostage.'

She gave him a withering look. 'Uzi, you are already a hostage!'

Uzi smiled and went back to the book.

By Friday evening black depression had settled over the terminal hall. Children had begun to cry while their mothers tried to cope with the growing fear in them as they saw so many adults sick and afraid. In an attempt to rouse people's spirits, Jean Jacques Maimoni collected sufficient water from the Ugandans to make tea and coffee, serving it to everyone together with the food that arrived.

There had been little contact with the terrorists since the morning, but Boese appeared in the evening with Tiedemann and the Arab, Al Arga, whose code name was 55. Itzhak David walked over to Boese, who was standing near the Davidson family watching the game of cards.

'Do you know what this is?' David asked him, showing Boese the number that was tattooed on his arm. 'It's from the concentration camps. The death camps of the holocaust.'

Boese, who had been keeping his distance

from the hostages since his early conversation with the lawer, Akiva Lexer, looked genuinely puzzled by the information.

'You understand me?' David asked him. 'My parents died in one of those camps.'

Boese shrugged uncomfortably. 'That's nothing to do with this.'

The old man gazed at him sadly. 'Then why are we here? Why did you segregate us so that now there are only Jews? It was that way before.'

'It was necessary,' said Boese.

'Yes, it was always necessary,' David answered bitterly. 'I'd thought that a new generation had grown up in Germany, but today when I see you and your girl friend it is difficult to believe that Nazism is dead.'

'I am not Nazi,' Boese replied. 'I am Baader Meinhof. We are fighting to free the world from capitalism.'

Sarah Davidson moved over to them and Michel Cojot, who could see that David was growing angry, also came over.

'So you are against capitalism,' David was saying, gesturing angrily towards the Arab by the door. 'If that is true, why do you collaborate with rich Arabs who want to kill ordinary working people who are innocent passengers.'

'I am anti-Nazi,' Boese said sharply.

Cojot intervened, worried lest David might lose his temper with the man. 'Surely you feel ill at ease,' he suggested gently. 'After all here you are, a German, taking Jews hostages thirty years after World War Two.'

'Our objectives are not the same as Hitler's,' Boese replied. 'Also the means are different. You know that we have been generous. Our behaviour is very correct.'

David snorted with disgust and waved a hand towards the toilets. 'We are living like pigs.'

Sarah Davidson agreed and told Boese that the conditions were very bad.

'It cannot be helped,' said Boese. 'If your government had agreed to our demands none of you would be here now.'

'You mean you'd have let the Jews go?' persisted David. 'The way you let the others go?'

Boese looked at him angrily and the Arab, Al Arga, moved towards them. 'Look, I understand the Jewish problem,' said Boese, 'but you should all try to understand the Palestinian problem.'

'They have no problem,' said Sarah. 'In 1948 they could have had a separate state. Since 1948 the Arab countries could have absorbed them, the way Israel has absorbed 600,000 Arabs.'

'That's not the way,' Boese said sharply. 'The Palestinians have a right to their own country.'

'And what about our country?' asked Sarah. 'Don't we have a right to a country of our own?'

'I have nothing against that,' Boese answered.

'Then why are you working with the Palestinians in this way,' she went on. 'You're an intelligent man, you understand things. What happens if you and your friends are successful? What happens if you do manage to drive us from Israel? Where will we go? Where will we live? In the sea?'

Boese gazed at her uncomfortably, then made a short, emphatic gesture. 'I am concerned with now. Not yesterday or tomorrow.'

'Then you should be concerned,' said Mrs Davidson. 'If you achieve the aims of the Palestinians we'll be without a country. Will you then go and catch planes for us – to find us a country?'

'Of course not,' Boese told her sharply.

The Arab, Al Arga, pushed forward with his gun in his hand. 'You twist things to suit yourselves,' he said in Hebrew. 'It's not our problem that Hitler killed six million Jews. You can't build a homeland on my land just to solve your problems.'

Boese refused to talk further, even though David attempted to continue the argument. The German walked away with Al Arga and after a moment Captain Bacos came over and spoke to them. This kind of conversation, he said, could only cause antagonism among the hijackers. He advised them not to raise the matter again. But Sarah Davidson, and many people who had witnessed the argument, believed that Boese had been acutely embarrassed by the analogy between his behaviour and that of the Nazis. Ilan Hartuv felt that Boese had never thought about it in those terms. The German had been obviously uncomfortable during the argument. For the first time since he had taken control of the aircraft, he had seemed uncertain.

Akiva Lexer spoke to him about the medical situation later and found him sharp and distant. Boese informed him coldly that he was not in charge and had no authority there. His authority had ended when he brought the Air France airbus into Entebbe. Later Lexer saw Boese and Tiedemann outside the terminal talking to the South American, Bouvier, who had arrived in a white Mercedes from Kampala. They stood together for about ten minutes, calling over the other terrorists to them.

Soon it was known that Bouvier had brought word from Kampala that the Israeli Government had agreed to release the prisoners named in the Palestinian ultimatum. The terrorists were delighted by the news, convinced that they had won a massive psychological victory over Israel. But in the main hall of the old terminal building, the mood was one of defeat and anguish. People were being sick, others were in pain, and few were finding it possible to sleep.

Sarah Davidson lay awake for most of the night, wondering at the way people were still able to live with the intolerable conditions and the fear. She decided that this was how it must have been in the concentration camps. No matter how bad things became, you continued to cherish the hope that tomorrow it would get better.

They had been told that the deadline expired on Sunday, but on Friday night she felt that something would have to happen before then. They could not live like this much longer.

Chapter 9

For Premier Yitzhak Rabin it was the hour of decision. Since 7 a.m. he had been meeting with his Minister of Defence, his Chief-of-Staff, and the key members of the Crisis Cabinet. It was now 10 a.m. and time was running out for everyone.

During the week, since his decision to negotiate with the terrorists, he had been reluctant to allow serious discussions on a military option. His reasons had been two-fold. In the first place he did not believe that such a venture could be achieved without considerable loss of life, in the second he was well aware of the political repercussions which would reverberate around the world against an Israel already losing friends and influence.

He knew that to launch such an operation, in spite of the responsibilities which would be shouldered by Shimon Peres and General Gur, would have to be his own decision and his alone.

94

He had the consolation of knowing that he would have the support of the opposition parties led by Menahem Begin, and he also knew that there were increasing doubts within the Knesset and the cabinet on the long-term effects capitulation to the PFLP would have on the negotiations being conducted to reach a settlement in the Middle East.

Such a capitulation would, in the eyes of many people, increase the isolation of Israel in the world. Such people also contended that the segregation of the Jews at Entebbe, and the freeing of the other passengers, had reaffirmed once more that Israel was the only target of the terrorists. There was grave apprehension in the minds of ministers and political advisers that the freeing of terrorist prisoners might not end the affair, and that, if the hostages were not released, this could lead to a confrontation between Israel and Uganda. The hijacking of the French airbus and the collusion of the Ugandan government were strengthening the view in Tel Aviv that Israel's intransigence in diplomacy and its refusal to allow other powers to advise or to act for it, was the only course the country could follow.

Although Rabin and his Cabinet had no proof that President Amin was privy to the hijacking, there was clear evidence of his complicity once the airbus had landed at Entebbe. This was established still more firmly by the fact that some of his personal bodyguards were Palestinian, and by the existence of PFLP bases in Uganda. The fact that this had not been condemned by the United Nations and that no pressure had been exerted on the Ugandan President was a further indication, if any were needed, of Israel's growing isolation. The cynical view was that the power of oil was able to override all other considerations, to the point where a criminal act of terrorism could be condoned on grounds of political expediency.

Yitzhak Rabin was not an eloquent man and he was probably the most cautious member of the cabinet. In recent years, and particularly since he had become Prime Minister, many of his opponents had accused him of being weak and indecisive. During the past forty-eight hours several members of the Crisis Cabinet had begun to lean towards the Minister of Defence and his military option. Yet the political consequences of such an act were daunting. Not only would there be an outburst of indignation from the Arab and Communist countries, but many of Israel's friends would find it difficult to condone an act of such open aggression.

His legal advisers were of the view that there was now sufficient evidence to show that

President Amin and his armed forces were in collusion with the PFLP. Under International Law, therefore, Israel would have the right to take limited action at Entebbe, providing it was for the sole purpose of rescuing Israeli citizens being held illegally in that country. Nevertheless, Premier Rabin was under no illusions as to the international condemnation the action would bring. If the operation was a failure, or resulted in a large number of casualties among the hostages as well as the attacking force, this condemnation would almost certainly mean the end of his political career. There was also the grave possibility that such an action could escalate into yet another war with the Arab world, at a time when they were patiently progressing towards a settlement.

The burden of responsibility was the heaviest that Premier Rabin had ever had to bear. He had spent many hours discussing the problem with his Foreign Minister, Yigal Allon, and with the various committees set up by the government to advise on such situations. Always the discussion came back to one inescapable fact. The PFLP were refusing to allow any supervision of the exchange by the United Nations. Many observers saw this as an indication that the hostages would never be released. Otherwise, it seemed there could be no reason for the hijackers to refuse to accept neutral territory for the transfer.

It was also pointed out that President Amin was a man who had proved time and time again that he could not be trusted. His brutal regime was credited with atrocities which made the killing of 100 hostages seem trivial by comparison. Above all else, he was a man ruled by mercurial emotions and a logic which few people could understand.

In the face of this knowledge Rabin told his Minister of Defence and Chief-of-Staff to outline their military option to his Crisis Cabinet. Quietly, without emotion, General Gur told them what the army intended to do.

As the plan unfolded the faces of the ministers came alive. Step by step the details of a most audacious and ingenious operation were laid before them. When General Gur had finished there was stunned silence, then a burst of applause.

Rabin sat at the head of the table, like a man of stone. Every eye turned towards him, waiting. He took a long, deep breath and tapped the table before him.

'I am in favour,' he said.

There was no need for a vote. An hour later the Premier briefed his full cabinet on the decision and received its support, but in Sharm el-Sheikh the final preparations were under way. In less than two hours, Operation Entebbe would no longer be a military option. It would be a reality.

Chapter 10

On Saturday morning General Gur ordered a
review of the entire operation, incorporating the
latest intelligence reports and the findings of the
air force. It began at 10 a.m. with a full briefing
of the unit commanders at Sharm el-Sheikh.
Brigadier-General Dan Shomron addressed the
force, now divided into the various tactical
groups which would carry out the specific tasks
allotted to them.

Present at the briefing were General Beni
Peled and General Yekuti Adam who would be
co-ordinating the force from the aerial command
post. The key to the operation, General Shomron
emphasized, was timing. Each move must be
carried out with precision, for if any unit went
into action even ten seconds too early it could
destroy the element of surprise essential to
success.

For this reason the aerial command post was
vital. Using advanced radar equipment, those

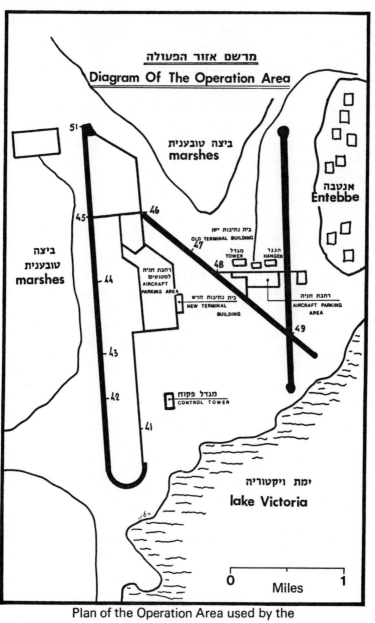

Plan of the Operation Area used by the
Israeli assault force

manning the post would be watching events below, and monitoring reports from agents in Kampala and around Entebbe. They would be in a position to activate each unit as it was required, their radar screens showing the developments on the ground.

'In this operation every second will count,' Shomron told them. 'Every man must know where and when to move.'

General Adam outlined the overall concept of the plan, describing how the three giant Hercules would swoop into Entebbe even as the Boeing 707 was lifting up above the airport and activating its radar jamming equipment. Each aircraft would carry units with a specific task. The first, which would land on the old runway, would carry Lieut.-Colonel Netanyahu and his men. This would be the first to touch down, using the confusion in the Entebbe radar room to cover its landing.

As the Hercules taxied towards the old terminal building, the other C130s would be touching down on the main runway. The intention was that the radar room and airport control personnel should believe, for the first minute or so, that these two aircraft were the Boeing, due from Nairobi, and an Israeli transport carrying the prisoners from Tel Aviv. During that minute the cargo doors would open and the jeeps, command cars and Israeli soldiers would emerge.

General Shomron took over, using a model and maps of Entebbe to show how the force he would lead would move towards the new terminal, splitting into two groups. The first would take the control tower and radar room, the second the terminal itself.

A third group, using two of the jeeps, would head for the squadrons of Migs parked on the far side of the airfield. It would be their task to deal with the Ugandan soldiers guarding the fighters and then to destroy the aircraft, effectively removing any retaliatory threat when they left Entebbe.

A fifth group, composed of one jeep and six men, would cross the airfield and join up with Israeli agents who had infiltrated the area after dark to set up an ambush on the road from the Ugandan Army camp. They would remain there until the operation had been completed, fighting a delaying action if necessary to prevent the Ugandans from reaching the airport.

Colonel Netanyahu outlined his operation, stressing the importance of taking the terminal in the first few minutes. The maximum time allocated for the complete evacuation of the hostages was 55 minutes, and they had estimated that the physical transfer of passengers to the Hercules could not be accomplished in less than twenty minutes. In addition to this were the delays in carrying wounded, checking the terminal building and ensuring that not one person had been left. This meant, in effect, that Colonel Netanyahu and his men must secure the building in ten minutes, evacuate in a further twenty, carry wounded and make the necessary checks in a further ten, then load the aircraft with the vehicles and his 80-strong force in the remaining twelve minutes.

It was a formidable task, for everyone knew that it would be taking place in the darkness under fire. It could only succeed if every man knew precisely where he was meant to be at any given time.

Many things were left unsaid at the briefing and during the rehearsal that followed. No one pointed out that if the airfield was not completely secured there would be very little chance of getting the giant C130s off the ground. It was equally obvious that the aircraft were extremely vulnerable while on the ground and even a single burst from a sub-machine-gun could put a Hercules out of action. If this happened, the plan was to abandon the jeeps and command cars, together with the armoured patrol car that Shomron's group would be using. Hostages and soldiers would cram into the remaining aircraft.

Although the men who made up Shomron's

force were the elite of Israel's army, few of them had experienced such a high degree of preparation. For many of them it was a disturbing experience. The full dress rehearsal took place in an area marked out with the dimensions of Entebbe, using some standing buildings as the old and new terminals and the control tower. Around these buildings Israeli troops took up the positions in which Intelligence reports indicated the defenders would be found. Using blank ammunition they fought a mock battle, resisting the attacking force in the way they believed the Ugandans would resist. Other soldiers played the part of the hostages, lying on the floor of the mock terminal building and waiting to be assisted from it to the waiting Hercules.

The aircraft themselves took up the positions they would occupy during the raid, the crews dragging out the refuelling equipment and hooking up to the fuel terminals. Medical teams, assigned to each aircraft, began to receive casualties and carry out mock operations within the first five minutes of the attack.

The disturbing feature for many of the men in that rehearsal was the large number of casualties being carried to the aircraft. General Gur and his staff had taken a pessimistic view, placing casualties deliberately high so as to assess the efficiency of a reduced force struggling to evacu-

105

ate under the most difficult conditions. For Shomron's men it was a constant reminder that the limp bodies being carried to the aircraft could be their own – a reality which was demonstrating the risks of battle with painful clarity. The tacticians had estimated a 40 per cent casualty rate – 30 dead, 50 seriously injured. Every other man in the task force could expect to be killed or wounded.

The heaviest of the casualties were envisaged as being concentrated around the old terminal building and involved Colonel Netanyahu's force, yet at no time was there any suggestion of concern amongst the members of that unit. Yoni led them forward, urging them into their respective positions, shouting to the hostages inside the building and then placing his men in defensive positions to cover the retreat to the aircraft. One after another men fell on the instructions of the observers and were carried on stretchers to the aircraft, but if any man wondered whether a real bullet would be waiting for him at Entebbe it never showed.

As one of the generals responsible for the tactical planning of the raid put it later, these were the most highly trained soldiers in Israel. The risks of battle were something they had come to terms with a long time ago. No matter what happened at Entebbe they would function to the maximum of their ability.

They were young men, supremely fit, capable of using any weapon – from a stripped down Uzi to the heavy Colt Commander automatic pistol. They could move stealthily in the darkness, communicating with each other by signs and sounds. They had learned how to survive in the harsh landscape of the Sinai and the treacherous ravines of the Golan Mountains.

This was the first time Shomron's men saw the full rehearsal of the manoeuvre which was to be the key to the entire operation. It was this, more than anything else, which infected every man with a sense of excitement. As the vehicles rolled out of the Hercules, crossing the five hundred yards of grass and concrete to the terminal building, it was all that many of the soldiers could do to keep from laughing. There was something incongruous in the procession of vehicles, in the knowledge that at Entebbe it would be a very courageous soldier indeed who would dare to open fire.

The rehearsal confirmed the complex strategy originally outlined in bulging briefing files. Here, for the first time, all the pieces of a tactical jigsaw puzzle fell into place. By noon the generals knew that the men could be deployed 45 seconds after landing, that the terminals could be taken and held, that it was possible for the hostages to be on board and taking off only 55 minutes after the first soldier emerged from the aircraft.

Even as they met in the large briefing room to hear the comments of Dan Shomron and his commanders, word came from Jerusalem that Rabin had approved the plan.

In his cool, laconic style, General Dan Shomron told his men: 'We go at 1600 hours and our ETA over Entebbe is 2300.'

Lieut.-Colonel Netanyahu had a further meeting with his generals, going over the latest intelligence reports from Uganda. They were encouraging. As General Gur had suspected all along, now that it appeared that they had won, the hijackers were beginning to get over-confident. They could not envisage any danger from the Israelis at Entebbe, so each day they were becoming more relaxed and less concerned about security at the airport. The Ugandan soldiers around the terminal were also reported to be bored and undisciplined.

President Amin was at the OAU Conference in Mauritius, preening himself before the assembled ministers, boasting openly of his triumph over Israel. Through the day he was completely unaware that his every move was being watched and reported back to Tel Aviv. Idi Amin was perhaps the most important piece in the tactical game of chess being played in

Israel. Throughout the night of 3 July the position of the Ugandan president would dictate the moves in Operation Entebbe.

And at Sharm el-Shiekh the giant Hercules were being given their final check in the hot Sinai sun. The vehicles were being loaded on board and Shomron's men were drawing grenades and ammunition, writing letters which were dropped casually into boxes with the rest of their belongings. With less than two hours to go, there wasn't a man at Sharm el-Sheikh who was not eager to be away.

Chapter 11

Whilst Shomron's men were chafing to be away,
Beni Peled and his commanders were meeting
with the meteorologists and getting bad news.
It was now confirmed that the deteriorating
weather between Israel and Uganda was settling
into a storm pattern which would be at its peak
during the flight to Entebbe. The storms would
slow down the Hercules and consume valuable
fuel, ruling out any chance of flying on to the
Seychelles. Unless they were able to refuel the
aircraft during the raid, and there was some
doubt about the feasibility of this, it was now
vital that the aircraft should land at Nairobi.

The responsibility for the transport of men,
equipment and hostages rested squarely on the
shoulders of Beni Peled. He was a vital, energetic
man who regularly piloted a Phantom jet fighter.
To his colleagues and friends he was, in every
sense, a professional soldier whose career ruled
his thinking and his life. During the Yom

Kippur War he had been addressing a Press Conference on the aerial aspects of the war when an aide had brought him a note. He read the message, then told the Press Conference that one of his pilots had been shot down. After answering questions for almost half an hour the conference broke up. One of the journalists, who knew him well, asked if he knew the name of the missing pilot.

'Yes, I do.' Peled replied calmly. 'It was my son.'

Later that day he was relieved to hear that his son had survived and was back with the Israeli forces, but the incident itself was an indication of the total dedication the general gave to his work.

On Saturday afternoon this strength enabled him to analyse the situation logically. He knew that the complex operation hinged on known activity in Ugandan airspace and at Entebbe Airport. Scheduled flights between Tel Aviv and Nairobi, and Nairobi and Entebbe, would be replaced by aircraft in the attacking force. To put back the operation would upset this intricate time-table and perhaps expose the aircraft to fighter attack or to evasive action on the ground at Entebbe.

This was the threat that everyone feared. Flying below the radar ceiling in storm conditions would inevitably tax the abilities of Peled's pilots to the maximum. He discussed it with them as they studied the weather maps, but each of his commanders assured him that they could still hold the tight formation and keep below the radar ceiling.

The flight over Ethiopia would be more difficult, the mountainous terrain severely handicapped the crews, but by that time they would be shielded from Saudi Arabian radar stations. Their route kept them well away from Addis Ababa, so they would have some room in the air once they cleared the Eritrean mountains.

The storms could prove to be an advantage, one of the commanders pointed out. In that kind of weather it would be unlikely that Egyptian or Saudi Arabian fighters would be in the air, and this would reduce the chances of an accidental sighting of the C130s. When the meeting ended General Peled informed General Gur and General Adam that take-off would be on schedule at 1600 hours.

Foreign Minister Allon and Defence Minister Peres, together with the Chief of Intelligence, Shlomo Gazit were told that the use of Nairobi was now inevitable. On Saturday afternoon messages went out to Israeli agents in Uganda and Kenya. It had long been agreed that Israel dared not take any other country into its confidence. The risks in making formal approaches to other governments were obvious. Agents in Kenya, however, had close contact with key officials in the city and at the airport. It was these officials who were to be approached in the next few hours, making them aware of the possibility of the emergency landing at Nairobi. They were also to make these officials aware that the Israelis would have no alternative but to seize the fuel terminal and airport facilities if this was the only way they could get back to Israel.

The Israeli Secret Service had been building up its agents in Kenya throughout the week. Whilst no one wanted to have recourse to an act of aggression, the request for assistance would now be backed up by a significant amount of muscle, not the least of which was a team of highly trained agents in the uniform of El Al crews.

In Jerusalem negotiations were continuing with the Palestinians through the French and Somali Ambassadors. The mood of these negotiations now changed, suggesting to the PFLP that Israel was ready and able to hand over the prisoners the following day. This information was also cabled to Paris and Bonn, where government ministers were told that arrangements would be made the following morning to collect the prisoners whom they would be handing over.

For the Germans it was a long and miserable night. The six prisoners they held in their jails were among the most hardened of the Baader Meinhof anarchists. When the country learned that they had been turned over to the PFLP there would be a bitter resentment which every observer had predicted would turn into a ballot-box backlash. Yet the German government had no doubt that in the last resort they must hand the prisoners over to the Israelis and leave it to them to do what they thought best.

In an attempt to discover if Israel was pursuing any alternative line, the French Ambassador, Jean Sauvagnargues, met Yigal Allon on Saturday. He found the Israeli Minister relaxed and helpful, apparently quite resigned to capitulating to the Palestinians and handing over the prisoners. He spent over an hour in the Foreign Minister's office but at no time did he suspect for a moment that the rescue operation was already on its way. Absolute secrecy was as vital a part of the Israeli plan as the strategy itself. On Saturday evening the Minister of Defence and the Chief-of-Staff attended a Barmitzvah party for the son of an army colleague, accepting the sympathy expressed by many of the guests at their inability to take some form of military action. Even as they drank and chatted to friends and army colleagues, their task force was almost half way to Entebbe. No one at the party had the slightest idea that there was any possibility of a rescue.

This was particularly true of one of the country's foremost soldiers, General Sharron. Sharron was the hero of the Yom Kippur War, a tough soldier who left the army to go into politics but found it not to his liking and had resigned to rejoin the army. There had been differences of opinion between General Sharron and Defence Minister Peres, a divergence of views which was, perhaps, heightened by the fact that the general's sojourn in politics had revealed that he had ambitions to take over the position of Minister of Defence. There had been rumours during the week that one of the hostages at Entebbe was none other than General Sharron himself and, although it had been denied in the Press, this was still widely believed in Tel Aviv.

On Saturday General Sharron, in one of his more acid moods, called out to Shimon Peres: 'With the speed that you are working I'm beginning to believe you really did think I was on that plane.' It was a remark that he would have cause to regret the following morning.

In Tel Aviv that night another party was in progress. This was being held at a large villa by the President of United Jewish Appeal. It was an occasion which would normally have been attended by all senior ministers and army generals, in particular General Gur's deputies, Beni Peled and Yekuti Adam.

More than a hundred guests were congregated around a swimming pool in the grounds of the villa, drinking cocktails and discussing the situation in Uganda. Shimon Peres appeared briefly, as did the Prime Minister, but there was a marked absence of generals. One of the guests, noticing this and realizing that such an absence could not be accidental, turned to a friend and said in a quiet, astounded voice. 'You know, it's incredible, but I think we could be up to something tonight.'

At that moment three C130s were skimming the waves of the Red Sea in tight formation, while 60,000 feet above them a flock of Phantoms were crawling through the night, every pilot watching his radar and the crimson horizons for the slightest sign of enemy fighters. General Peled and General Adam, whose absence at the party had been noted 'with regret', were on board a Boeing 707 with an official flight plan listing it as unscheduled flight LY 167 to Nairobi. The aircraft was flying at the normal cruising height of 30,000 feet along the Red Sea and across Ethiopia for Kenya. Radar posts in Egypt, Saudi Arabia and Ethiopia noticed nothing unusual about the blip on their screens. In fact, throughout the entire journey, no one suspected that there were actually two Boeings.

The first was LY 167, the Israeli mobile hospital which would land at Nairobi on schedule. The second had the military registration number, 4XBY8, and was listed as Flight LY 169. By flying in close formation the radar stations below could not separate the two aircraft, and no one was to know that a unique aerial command post crammed with sophisticated electronics was already halfway to Uganda.

Chapter 12

In many ways the aerial command post was the key to the Israeli operation. It had been General Peled's first thought when told of the need for a military option. Getting the force in and out of Entebbe was one thing, but co-ordinating them on the ground without interference or confusion was essential if the attack were to be carried out with speed and efficiency.

'I can operate in the air above Entebbe,' he had told General Gur five days ago. 'I can be invisible to their radar, in contact with agents in Kampala and the forces on the ground.'

Not only that, an aerial command ship would form a vital communications link with Tel Aviv, so that General Gur and his staff could listen to the complete operation, communicating with General Shomron and his commanders on the ground via the Boeing if this became necessary.

Having promised the impossible, Beni Peled had to devise the means and the ways of carrying it out. The interior of the military Boeing 707 had been stripped and equipped with a large plotting table with the operational area of Entebbe illuminated beneath plastic. The positions of each unit on the ground could be plotted, drawn or marked with symbols, with General Adam, the Chief-of-Staff's second in command, co-ordinating the movements with General Gur in Tel Aviv and General Shomron on the ground below.

Lining the fuselage on either side of the operations table were the telecommunications decks. High Frequency radio provided a two-way link with Military Headquarters in Tel Aviv, more than 2000 miles away. This 'point-to-point' circuit was scrambled to prevent any chance operator from listening in, but to add further protection the communications operator was also using a system known as 'single side band'.

This system cannot be detected by radio monitoring stations because the signal's carrier wave is cancelled out before transmission and replaced electronically at the receiving end. With only the side band of the wavelength being transmitted it is more effective, requires less power, and cannot be received by anyone else.

The second communications link was VHF, ground to air, enabling Israeli Secret Service agents in Kampala and the area around Entebbe to speak directly to General Adam 30,000 feet above on simple 'line of sight' handsets. This second communications officer had a technical back-up man who was able to link the ground-to-air communications directly into the HF link with Tel Aviv.

A third communications operator manned a bank of receivers, monitoring communications in Entebbe, Kampala, and Nairobi. Throughout the flight to Entebbe, and during the actual operation, this man listened to the air waves and was not even aware of the progress of the operation below.

But one man was acutely aware of it. He was a senior radar operator, an acknowledged expert in airborne radar, and together with a technical assistant, he used a sophisticated 8 mm radar scan which operated through a 90 degree arc to cover the entire airport 30,000 feet below. This equipment had built-in features enabling the operator to angle it to reveal contours, buildings and large objects such as aircraft. In this way Peled and Adam were able to watch the C130s land on the runways far below and take up their positions. It also showed the precise locations of the squadrons of Mig fighters, confirming the information Intelligence had been communicating throughout the day. During the attack this operator was able to switch ranges, sweeping up to 30 miles to cover Kampala, and narrowing the range down to five miles to encompass the perimeter of Entebbe Airport.

The electronics were only part of the wizardry that Beni Peled's telecommunications staff had come up with. The Israelis, having virtually built Entebbe Airport, had precise information about the equipment being used there. They knew, for instance, that the approach frequency was 119.1 megacycles, and that radar cover was provided by a Plessey AR1. This enabled them to plot the neutral zone which exists directly above the transmitting dish on all primary radar. In the case of the AR1 in use at Entebbe, it meant that Beni Peled's technical team knew that a cone extended above the airport which, at 30,000 feet, gave a blind zone sixteen miles wide. The Boeing, which could execute a circle with a radius of five miles, was able to operate within this cone without radar detection by Entebbe.

The problem was, how could Beni Peled get his command post into this cone. Again, knowledge of the Entebbe equipment provided the answer. The Israeli radar experts calculated what in technical circles is called 'blind speed'; the speed, in effect, at which aircraft will not register on the primary radar equipment used at many airports, including Entebbe.

The Boeing would approach on the normal glide path, identifying itself as a flight from Nairobi, and eight miles from the runway would change its speed from 200 knots to 296. In the Uganda radar room the effect would be little short of miraculous. At 296 knots the Boeing would disappear from the radar screen. It would then leave the glide path, holding its speed to 296 knots, climbing up in little more than two minutes to the 'blind cone' where it could circle at any speed and be invisible to the radar below.

This manoeuvre, baffling even for General Gur and his staff, placed a highly sophisticated command post above Entebbe whilst the radar operators were still desperately trying to find out what had happened to the Boeing from Nairobi. At that precise moment another blip would appear on the radar screen and announce itself as a special military flight from Tel Aviv bearing the prisoners requested by President Idi Amin. On the radar screen the single blip would conceal the fact that it was two C130s, in position on the glide path at a height of 2500 feet, and only one minute from touch down.

The third C130, which was still flying low beneath the radar cover, would be taking up its position to land on the airport's old runway. Even as its wheels were touching the runway, and in the control tower a mile away the

Ugandan radar operators were frantically trying to work out what was happening, the command Boeing above would be switching on its radar jamming device and Israeli agents around the airfield detonating charges which would cut every line of communication with Kampala.

After four days of planning Beni Peled's technical team had put the force in Entebbe, ready to go into action, and the only indication on the Ugandan radar screens had been a single blip which appeared to be one aircraft coming in to land. Even while the bewildered operators were trying to discover if the African Airways Boeing 707 had crashed into Lake Victoria, Israeli agents were talking to General Adam on VHF and all the telephone lines were going dead.

Operation Entebbe had begun.

Chapter 13

Saturday was the Sabbath and the worst day, by far, for the hostages. Without water and racked with diarrhoea, everyone in the terminal began to sink into a stupor of pain and despair.

The ground floor of the building, of which the main hall was occupied by the hostages, had only six toilets for more than a hundred people. Without water the stench became appalling. By mid-morning conditions were becoming impossible to endure and some of the elderly people had begun to slip into delirium. Others were unable to move from where they lay, vomiting and racked with pain.

Captain Bacos was incensed by the conditions and spoke to the Palestinians and the Ugandans, insisting on medical attention. The doctor who had previously been responsible for the hostages and who had admitted Mrs Bloch into the hospital in Kampala, had not been seen since. There were rumours that his concern for a hostage had been viewed with displeasure by the military and Amin's secret police.

Without a doctor there was serious danger of a complete breakdown in the health of the hostages, and the lack of water was heightening the suffering. The pots of badly-cooked meat and the interminable rice and bananas were largely untouched and the soft drinks brought by the Ugandans provided only a brief solace. As though to enhance the fear in everyone's mind, the Ugandans brought the Air France airbus back to the terminal, parking it beside the building.

For many this was the most devastating proof that President Amin's grim warning of the previous day was about to be fulfilled. The terrorists had mentioned on more than one occasion that the airliner was mined with explosives, and Wilfred Boese had made no secret of the fact that he wanted to blow it up. On Saturday, in the hot, foetid air of the terminal which even the Palestinians were reluctant to enter, the despairing hostages felt that the end was very near.

For young Nadia Israel it was an endless nightmare. Her mother, the pretty flat in Netanya with its cool balcony, the children who always seemed to be playing happily below, seemed part of another world that had gone for ever. The slim elfin-faced girl with long black hair was now pale and gaunt. Her large brown eyes were haunted by the fear and suffering around her. Only her aunt, Nina Zehren, and the Davidson family who never stopped playing cards, kept this nightmare world at bay.

That morning they watched Boese and Tiedemann meet Bouvier on the tarmac outside the terminal. Bouvier, the elegant South American, was grim and troubled. They spoke for half an hour, and then the airliner was brought to the terminal.

Fear engulfed Nadia. How easy it would be, she thought, to put us all on board and tell us we are going home. Then press a button and blow us all away. The same thought was in many people's minds, and the glib assurances of Boese when he spoke to them did little to quell their fear. For six days now they had heard these assurances, felt their spirits lift, only to find that next day was worse than the day before and there was no sign of their release.

Captain Bacos frequently walked around the room, speaking quietly to the small, lethargic groups. Without his strength 'and calm conviction that everything would be all right, many would have given up that day. As it was there were some who retreated into that limbo of the mind where nothing more could be felt.

But Nadia clung to those around her. It was Uzi Davidson's unemotional acceptance of everything that had happened since they arrived at Entebbe which gave her the most profound feeling that this was, somehow, as Uzi said: 'A passing moment'. Uzi Davidson was a phlegmatic man who regarded emotion with a certain degree of contempt. His wife, Sarah, was in complete contrast and was frequently exasperated by his lack of sensitivity, but in this alien world it was a source of strength for the entire group.

'I don't know what you're getting so upset about,' said Uzi. 'It's nothing. Tomorrow you'll laugh about it.'

It was this attitude which carried them through the day. At one point he was asked how he could be so detached, so unconcerned about the plight of his family, if not himself. Uzi Davidson smiled wryly and said he would have been far more concerned if his family had been at home in Israel. Then he would have worried all the time about their fears, the torment that would have been with them while his captivity lasted.

'I have my family around me,' he said, 'and that is all that matters.'

In spite of the danger and sickness, Uzi never doubted that something would happen soon. His conviction infected those around him and the

Davidson family were often strengthened by it.

The family, the group, the sharing of the deprivation, were the things that held most of the hostages together on that Saturday. And there were many who did their utmost to bolster the falling spirits of the elderly and the young.

Mrs Ruth Gross, the schoolteacher, continued to help the children in spite of her own sickness. Moshe Peretz, a medical student from Tel Aviv, did what he could for the worst of the sufferers, but without water or drugs the help could only be psychological. Akiva Lexer, the lawyer, encouraged many to continue playing cards and draughts, and Jean-Jacques Maimoni spent the morning comforting an elderly woman who was unable to move and continuously vomiting.

But the complaints by Captain Bacos about deteriorating conditions in the terminal had finally penetrated the muddled bureaucracy of the Ugandans. Two army doctors were sent with instructions to alleviate the suffering of the hostages. When they arrived they immediately recognized the dangers of a major epidemic and called for airport staff to clean out the toilets. Then they set about administering medicine. The more seriously ill were injected with sedatives in addition to medicines which could arrest the condition while the remainder received pills or a mixture of kaolin and morphine. A few were taken to an army clinic for treatment, but this proved a largely futile exercise.

When the pots of meat, rice and bananas arrived at noon there were few who could eat, but the severe pains had begun to ease as the drugs began to take effect. Those who had received sedatives were either sleeping or drowsy, and many of the children were too exhausted to be interested in food. Only the lukewarm soft drinks were in demand, and Maimoni was one of the helpers who made sure that everyone who was awake received a bottle.

In the afternoon, as though in an attempt to cheer up the depressed hostages, the Ugandans delivered a truck-load of pillows. There were enough for everyone, but for some the unexpected gift was fresh cause for alarm. It seemed to suggest that the Ugandans were beginning to make more permanent arrangements. Nevertheless, since the first time they arrived in Entebbe, people were able to relax on the mattresses with some degree of comfort.

Gabrielle Tiedemann spent more time in the room with them than any other of the terrorists, and at the height of the sickness she seemed to obtain a certain degree of satisfaction from the suffering around her. Elia Lipsky was one of the people who felt that the two German members of the gang seemed to be under increasing pressure.

129

It was reflected in the tight, distant manner of Boese and the way he kept to himself on the tarmac outside the building. It was also demonstrated by Tiedemann's manner towards the Israelis. She had become known as the 'Nazi Bitch' and was cruel at the best of times, but on Saturday she spent more time than ever strutting around with a pistol in her hand, sneering at the misery of the hostages. A child began to cry and this clearly irritated the woman. She ordered the child to be quiet and, when he continued to cry, slapped him hard across the face.

The Israelis watched with helpless anger, knowing that the slightest sign of resistance would be all the provocation that Tiedemann would need. The brutal forces which drove the woman were never more in evidence than on Saturday. At the height of the suffering and misery she was in her element.

In contrast, Wilfred Boese appeared to have no liking for what he saw. He kept away from the hostages as much as possible, sitting outside against the wall of the terminal. Sarah Davidson, who had obtained permission to take her youngest son outside for some fresh air, went over and spoke to him about the conditions.

He told her that there was nothing he could do. He had no authority at the terminal, but he was sure that the Ugandans would do what they could. With the disarming smile he had used so often during the week, he assured Sarah that there was really nothing to worry about.

'It won't be long now,' he said. 'By this time tomorrow I'm sure you'll be on your way home.'

In the early days at Entebbe, Sarah had found it easy to believe the young German but this was no longer the case. She returned to the terminal, full of doubts, wondering how she could cope with tomorrow if the promised freedom did not come. Ron was playing cards and Uzi was reading his book, so she said nothing. Instead she busied herself with rearranging their mattresses and pillows, consolidating the small area of the main hall which she called 'their little nest'.

Benji was playing with a friend. Suddenly, with a very serious expression, he said that they were going to be rescued. Sarah looked at him in surprise, struck by the gravity of the boy.

'What do you mean?' asked the friend.

Benji frowned, looking puzzled. 'I don't know. I just have a feeling that we're going to be rescued.'

The friend was sceptical, but Benji persisted. 'We'll be rescued by the army,' he said. 'I just know we will.'

Sarah felt close to tears. She did not have

the heart to tell him that such a rescue was impossible. Their soldiers were more than two thousand miles away and this was a hostile country. To Benji it was simple. The commandos would come and take them home. But to Sarah Davidson it was an impossible dream.

At that very moment, three Hercules were taking off from Sharm el-Sheikh. The commandos were on their way.

There were small improvements during the afternoon and evening. Most of the hostages were making rapid recoveries and beginning to cheer up, and the Ugandans had begun to increase the water supply so that tea and coffee could be made again. Pasco Cohen and Jean-Jacques Maimoni took charge of this and provided hot drinks for everyone.

They had been told throughout the day that President Amin would be visiting them, and at five o'clock he arrived in his Mercedes wearing an air force uniform decorated with Israeli parachute wings. Beaming cheerfully at the attentive hostages, he told them that there would be a solution very soon.

'I am doing everything I can,' he said. 'At this moment I have arrived from Mauritius where, as you know, I am President of the Organization for African Unity. We have been discussing your situation. I have been discussing it with the Palestinians and with the French. You can be sure that I am doing everything I can to save your lives.'

He held out his arms as though to embrace them all. 'I am like a father to you,' he said proudly, 'and it is your own government which is to blame. If they do not accept the terrorist demands by noon tomorrow, it will be their fault. Not mine. Not the Palestinians. The Palestinians are only doing what they must.'

There was silence in the room. The message was very clear and many faces reflected the fear his words evoked. Then the President's mood changed and he was beaming again, reassuring them that their ordeal would soon be over.

'It will end tomorrow,' he said. 'You have my word, there will be a solution tomorrow.'

But after President Amin had left there were many who wondered privately, and with apprehension, what that solution would be.

The evening dragged on and darkness fell. Outside, the Ugandans switched on the brilliant lights which illuminated the tarmac around the terminal. Some of the hostages, still drowsy from the sedatives, were dozing, but others were gathering in groups and talking. The Davidsons, with Pasco Cohen, had begun a game of bridge.

Suddenly, for no apparent reason, the mood

133

changed. Someone suggested a game and small groups around the room took it up. The game was inventing the headlines that day for the newspapers back home in Israel. Each of the newspapers has its own style and approach, some subtle, others extreme. In minutes the old airport lounge was full of laughter. First one suggestion was put forward, then embellished by another.

They laughed as one man suggested the headline for a newspaper given to exaggeration: 'Hostages Seize Uganda'.

'No, no,' he was corrected. 'Hostages *Buy* Uganda!'

Then came another idea, that had everyone roaring with laughter: 'Amin Buys Banana Plantation'.

The game went on for almost an hour, then people began to talk with hope again.

Boese and Tiedemann, who seemed irritated by the amusement, went out on to the tarmac and began talking to a group of Ugandan officers, whilst three of the hijackers went upstairs to the roof terrace where a detachment of Ugandan soldiers took up position each night. There was always a plentiful supply of beer on the roof terrace, and as the night wore on there were the sounds of drunken laughter from above.

Along the tarmac from the terminal building other soldiers were on duty in the old control tower, occasionally shouting to the Ugandans patrolling the perimeter. There were some 120 soldiers in various positions in and around the buildings, but their attitude was one of casual boredom. It was a necessary chore, just in case Amin returned unexpectedly, but neither the terrorists nor the Ugandans believed for one moment that there was any danger of an attack.

Bouvier and two of the senior PFLP members were at the palace with President Amin, keeping in touch with the French and Somali Ambassadors. They were awaiting news of the arrival of the prisoners from Israel, which they had been told was scheduled for the following morning.

In the main hall of the terminal the 104 remaining passengers and the crew were bedding down for the night. Some of them continued to play cards, including the Davidson family who were still absorbed in their game of bridge. One group, close to the long window overlooking the tarmac, were involved in a heated argument about the attitude of the hijackers. They were divided on the question of whether or not the hijackers were bluffing: whether they would be prepared to kill the hostages if Israel did not release the prisoners by noon next day. The casual attitude of the Ugandan soldiers outside led some of them to believe that they were nowhere near a crisis and that the negotiations could drag on for weeks. Others pointed to the grim warnings by Amin, and the way Tiedemann and the Palestinians had seemed particularly callous that day.

It was a depressing argument and no one voiced the thought that was at the back of everyone's mind. If the prisoners were delivered on schedule, would the hijackers even then allow them to leave? In spite of the assurances by Boese, there was no indication of this in the attitudes of the other hijackers. The group began to break up. It was midnight in Uganda, eleven o'clock in Tel Aviv.

Nadia Israel was trying to get to sleep, her young aunt, Nina, already asleep beside her.

Jean-Jacques Maimoni was sitting by the window, looking across the tarmac, watching the soldiers leaning on their guns and talking idly with each other.

Sarah Davidson wanted to get to sleep, but Benji and Ron were cheerfully planning to play all night.

Captain Bacos was with his crew, most of them asleep. They had been talking quietly about tomorrow and what it would bring. He looked around the dimly-lit room, relieved that the worst of the sickness appeared to be over.

By the window Jean-Jacques Maimoni got to his feet and went to his mattress in the centre of the room, picking his way carefully among the sleeping families. He lay down and closed his eyes. He was asleep almost immediately.

Across the airfield, less than a mile away, the modern terminal and control tower were brightly lit, the guards oblivious to the fact that in the darkness Israeli agents were moving silently into position. Explosive charges, taped to telephone and telex cables, were primed and ready to be detonated.

And thirty thousand feet above Entebbe two generals were watching a glowing radar screen. Beyond them the telecommunications men were hunched over their transmitters. Below, skimming the waters of Lake Victoria, were three giant Hercules.

The time was one minute past midnight.

Chapter 14

'This is El Al Flight 166 with the prisoners from Tel Aviv,' said the Israeli pilot in a quiet, laconic voice. 'Can I have permission to land?'

The C130 was three minutes from touchdown showing clearly on the glide path in the Entebbe Control Tower. What did not show was the fact that there were two aircraft, side by side, coming in over Lake Victoria.

There were three air traffic controllers on duty at Entebbe, and they were completely bewildered by the sudden inexplicable chain of events. Badrew Muhindi and Tobias Rwengeme were trying to locate the African Airways flight from Nairobi which had vanished from their radar screens, while Lawrence Mawenda was endeavouring to contact the Civil Aviation Director, Peter Kalanzi, and getting no reply.

In desperation the air traffic controllers grabbed telephones and tried to call Kampala for instructions, but every line was dead. They could only watch with numbed disbelief, as two air-craft came out of the night and touched down on the main runway. They were not civil aircraft at all but huge, camouflaged military transports.

Across the airfield, hidden by rising ground, the third of the giant Hercules was touching down on the disused runway. The pilot, using the brilliantly-lit old terminal as a beacon and switching on his landing lights at the last possible moment, placed the C130 firmly on the pot-holed runway and reversed the four powerful Allison D22A turboprops. The Hercules had the shortest landing distance for any aircraft in the world of comparable size, and less than thirty seconds after touchdown it was turning off the runway and taxi-ing towards the old terminal.

Inside, Lieut.-Colonel Yonatan Netanyahu took up his position beside the cargo ramp, glancing back along the crouching ranks of men. Only their eyes gleamed in the darkness. The lights had been extinguished for almost an hour now so that they were all fully accustomed to the dark.

It had been a far from pleasant journey, lasting seven hours, and for much of that time they had been buffeted by head winds and storms over the Red Sea. After the first hour many of the men had begun to suffer from nausea and this persisted until they were clear of the mountains of Ethiopia five hours later.

But the men were hardened soldiers and the discomfort only served to take their minds off the ever-present danger of the sea beneath them. In spite of the storms, the C130 pilots held the huge aircraft low beneath the radar cover of the neighbouring countries. Such a manoeuvre would have been impossible had it not been for the sophisticated flight control equipment which constantly corrected the height and course of the aircraft. To have lifted up above the storm would have meant revealing their positions to Egypt, Libya, Saudi Arabia and the Sudan. Long before they reached Entebbe, the Ugandan Army would have been on full alert and waiting for them.

Instead the giant C130s thundered through the howling winds, only a few hundred feet above the angry sea, their engines at maximum revs to hold a cruising speed of 350 mph. Above them, well clear of the storm, were two squadrons of Phantom F4 fighters, armed with Sidewinder missiles. With their radar systems they were able to watch the entire area around the Red Sea, ready to go into action the moment Arab fighters threatened the task force below.

The pilots who flew the Hercules were among the finest in Israel's Air Force, but for the first 1500 miles it took all their courage and experience to hold the giant transports in tight formation through the turbulence. Long before they reached Ethiopia the Phantoms above were peeling away and heading back for Israel, their range exhausted. For the next six hours the fighter pilots would sweat it out at Sharm el-Sheikh, ready to take off at any moment to protect the returning aircraft.

As the Phantoms pulled out, two Boeings were falling into position above the Hercules at a height of 33,000 feet. This was one of the trouble spots; the last few hundred miles along the Red Sea before the C130s could turn inland and begin cutting through the valleys and ravines of Ethiopia. The flight plan of the Boeings, which were registering as a single aircraft on the area radar, coincided with the task force for one hour before their faster speed took them away.

The planning team had calculated that this discrepancy of speed, some 75 miles per hour, would enable the Boeings to be above the C130s for 300 miles before they turned inland over Ethiopia. For this period they had calculated that the radar posts along the Red Sea would be watching 'Flight LY 169' on course for Nairobi and would fail to notice the brief period – less than four sweeps of a radar scope – when the Hercules lifted up and over the first ridge of the

Eritrean mountains between Massawa and Port Sudan. A strike by radar technicians in the Sudan was an unexpected bonus for the Israelis, who learned hours before the flight that only one out of three radar stations was being manned.

As the C130s slipped down the valleys and ravines towards Lake Rudolph on the border of Kenya, the Boeings were holding their scheduled course across Ethiopia at a height of 33,000 feet. The leading Boeing, LY 169, maintained radio contact with area traffic controllers, proceeding in a perfectly innocent fashion towards Nairobi. Only when they were descending towards the mountains beyond Nanyuki did Beni Peled's Boeing peel away and head in a wide, four hundred mile circle for Lake Victoria, timing its arrival to coincide with the C130s who had cut straight across from Lake Rudolph to Kakamega.

It was this precision flying which put the task force together in one spot in the middle of Africa at midnight local time, and the only people who had the slightest indication of what was happening were the radar operators at Nairobi Airport. Their area radar extended to Entebbe and they had watched, with some bewilderment, the unidentified Boeing approach Entebbe and then suddenly climb to 30,000 feet. When it became stationary on their radar screens they knew the

Boeing was circling within the 'blind cone' above the airport. After that, the appearance of three more aircraft came as no surprise, nor did their disappearance from the screens which indicated that they had landed.

Few Kenyans had reason to like President Idi Amin. For years their countrymen in Uganda had been persecuted, and for the past year the Ugandan Radio had been making threats against Kenya, including arbitrary territorial claims involving a large section of Kenya beside Lake Victoria. Nor did the Ugandan association with the Palestinians make them more popular in Kenya, especially since, only a few months before, a Palestinian plot at Nairobi Airport had been foiled with Israeli help. It was not surprising, therefore, that at midnight on Saturday a number of Kenyans watched what was happening with a certain satisfaction.

For Colonel Netanyahu's men the problem had always been how to get close enough to the old terminal. Although discipline around the building was lax, the Israelis were under no illusions about the Palestinian reaction to an attack. They would kill as many of the hostages as possible.

The early plans, which had ranged from parachute drops in the dark to a Boeing 707 packed with commandos disguised as prisoners, had all been rejected because they did not fulfil the primary requirement of putting the Israeli force close enough to the terrorists to prevent retaliation on the hostages.

At first the tactical problems had appeared insoluble. More than a hundred well-armed Ugandan soldiers, spread around the terminal and on the roof terrace, made storming the building out of the question. A landing on the main runway, almost a mile away, would give the Ugandans ample time to take cover and open fire with automatic rifles and machine-guns. To attack across brilliantly-lit open ground, in the face of such a fusillade, would be suicidal. The Israelis would be pinned down before they got half way, and with the Ugandans in commanding positions and able to call on reserves from the nearby army camp, the chances of ever reaching the terminal were remote.

Only an overwhelming force capable of sustaining heavy casualties could make such an attack feasible, and Yoni's group was anything but that. His men numbered no more than fifty tough young commandos, crouching now in the wide body of the Hercules with safety catches off.

The final solution had been a plan so audacious that it would catch the Ugandans and the hijackers completely off their guard. It was the key to the entire Israeli operation and its essential element sat now between the men, gleaming in the darkness, the engine already purring as the Hercules taxied to the edge of the tarmac facing the old terminal; a large black Mercedes complete with an escort of two British Land-Rovers. In the driving seats of the Mercedes and the Land-Rovers were Israelis with blackened hands and faces. It had been decided, because Amin's Mercedes had curtained windows, that it would be unnecessary to have a fake President in the car. Instead, behind the drawn curtains, two paratroopers crouched with Galil assault rifles. In the back of the two Land-Rovers were men very similar to the President's Palestinian bodyguards.

The Hercules came to a halt, and the heavy ramp slowly lowered itself to the ground.

'Go,' said the commander.

The first Land-Rover accelerated down the ramp, out on to the brilliantly-lit tarmac followed immediately by the Mercedes and the second Land-Rover.

Gabrielle Tiedemann and Wilfred Boese were standing outside the door of the terminal talking to a young Ugandan officer when the C130 came to a stop five hundred yards away. They watched with some surprise as the huge aircraft swung itself round, then opened its cargo hold.

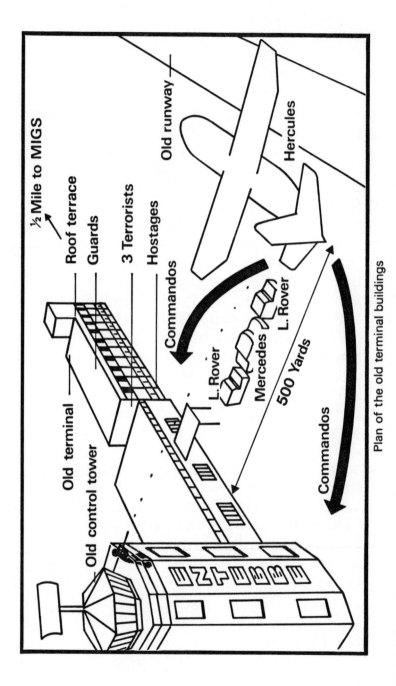

Plan of the old terminal buildings

Beyond them, scattered across the tarmac in front of the terminal, Ugandan soldiers turned to face the aircraft which had come to a halt on the edge of the illuminated area. It had scarcely stopped when the ramp was coming down and the vehicles roared out on to the tarmac. Without hesitation the soldiers snapped to attention.

The escort Land-Rovers and the Mercedes swept towards them at a steady pace, the guards sitting casually in the rear of the vehicles. No one doubted the evidence clearly before them, that President Amin was arriving for another meeting with the hostages and hijackers. Those who had time to think about the giant military transport simply assumed that he had arrived from the OAU conference in Mauritius. Only Boese and Tiedemann found this unlikely, and as the Mercedes with its escorts came closer, Boese turned and went into the terminal, collecting his sub-machine-gun from where it was leaning against the wall.

By this time the convoy was among the Ugandans and coming to a stop. One soldier, close to the lead Land-Rover and some ninety yards from the terminal building, suddenly realized that the men he had assumed were Palestinians were wielding Uzi sub-machine-guns, not the Russian Kalichikofs they normally carried. With a shout of alarm he raised his gun, realizing immediately that he had seen none of these men before.

That Ugandan soldier was the first man to die at Entebbe.

Even as the first wave of gunfire broke out, Yoni's men were lunging down the ramp of the Hercules and racing for the terminal. This was the exercise they had rehearsed again and again until they could empty the aircraft and fan out into position in forty-five seconds. The training paid off. Even as the astonished Ugandans were trying to recover, Israeli commandos were racing across the tarmac, firing short bursts from the Uzi sub-machine-guns.

Around the Mercedes it was chaos. The men in the Land-Rovers were laying down a withering fire on all sides. In the Mercedes itself were commandos equipped with Galil assault rifles, sweeping the area with high velocity automatic fire. In the leading Land-Rover the driver was methodically shooting out the brilliant lights along the roof of the terminal.

It was all too much for those Ugandan soldiers that were still on their feet after that first, shattering, minute. They turned and ran for the darkness, only to find Israelis coming in on either side in a flanking movement. The attack was total and terrifying, the area in front of the

148

terminal already littered with wounded and dying men.

Gabrielle Tiedemann saw it all, at first with disbelief, then with rage. She raised her pistol, aiming at the lean young men racing towards the terminal. She fired one shot, and was then cut down by a hail of bullets from the converging Israelis.

In the passage leading to the main hall of the terminal, Wilfred Boese was desperately trying to find the magazine for his sub-machine-gun. He had left it by the doorway of the room containing the hostages. The sound of shooting and the cries of Ugandans were deafening. He was only dimly aware of the quick bursts of fire outside the building, of the lights beginning to go out. He found the magazine, slapped it into his gun and cocked it. Facing him was the door to the lounge; behind him the passage and tarmac beyond, echoing to the snarl of machine-guns.

Boese knew what he must do. He stepped into the main hall, his gun aimed at the helpless hostages. Many of them were still asleep, others just beginning to react to the gunfire outside. A few were starting to cry out, huddling down on the floor. A few feet away from him was a man he recognized as Ilan Hartuv. They stared at each other and Boese hesitated, his finger on the trigger, a hundred helpless people before him.

Then he turned and ran from the room into the passage. Ahead was the tarmac, now lit dimly by one remaining light. The night was laced with stroboscopic flashes from a dozen sub-machine-guns. He ran towards the door, lunging out with the gun rising in his hands.

The bursts of gunfire which killed Wilfred Boese came from every side.

Colonel Netanyahu was at the head of the first group of men who raced into the terminal. The Israelis, firing from the vehicles on the tarmac, had effectively pinned down or eliminated the detachment of soldiers guarding the front of the building, but there were still the detachment on the roof terrace and the Ugandans in the old control tower.

Netanyahu paused at the doorway to the passageway that connected with the stairs and the ground floor area. His mind was ticking off the seconds, separating each task and analysing the time and men needed to accomplish it. A few feet away lay the bodies of the two Germans, but there were at least eight other hijackers somewhere in the building. On his left an Israeli had jumped on to the ledge of the window looking into the main hall, holding himself there with his left hand whilst his right swept the Uzi, ready for any sign of resistance. The man seemed completely unconcerned that he would be a clear target for any terrorist in that room. With almost ludicrous calm, he asked in Hebrew if there were any terrorists in the room. Another Israeli, using a loud-hailer, was already shouting to the hostages in the terminal. '*Tishkavu, tishkavu,*' he called urgently. Lie down, lie down.

Even as these sounds and images were registering in Yoni's mind, he was checking the men with him beside the doorway. A brief nod, a flick of the hand, and then he was lunging into the darkened passage and running for the stairs. They ran silently, in desert boots that whispered on the concrete. The stairs turned, became a short hall with a cracked green door. From the roof terrace beyond came the sound of firing. Yoni flattened against the wall on the left side of the door, nodded to the two men who were against the wall on the opposite side. They unhooked grenades, pulled the pins, crouching. He stepped back, kicked at the door which burst inwards, and then was back against the wall.

A burst of shots came from the room, but they found nothing but an empty doorway. The two grenades bounced across the room, clattering briefly on the floor. The three Palestinians crouching behind a stack of aircraft seats cried out and tried to reach the window opening on to the roof. It was a mistake. The grenades detonated with a deafening roar in the narrow confines of the concrete room, the deadly shrapnel ricocheting off walls, ripping through the expensive upholstery of Idi Amin's luxury aircraft seats and into the bodies of Jail El Arga and the two Arabs who had been known for seven days as 39 and 55. Even as they were falling, Yoni and his men were stepping into the room and sweeping it with bursts of 9mm from the Uzi sub-machine-guns.

Outside, on the tarmac, an Israeli officer was speaking softly into his radio, the aerial pointing directly overhead.

'We are in the terminal,' he said. 'Yoni is going for the roof.'

Around the huge C130 men were lying motionless on the ground, Galil assault rifles and high magnification night-sights sweeping the darkness of the airfield. Many Ugandan soldiers had run off into the night, but, if they regrouped and attacked, the aircraft would make a large and extremely vulnerable target.

Other Israelis were behind the terminal building, and it was this group that caught two Palestinians running from the building. One of them was Haj Faiz Gaber, the most senior member of the PFLP at Entebbe. Both men died swiftly, running from the sound of gunfire.

In the terminal itself Israelis were entering

from the passage, the side door and the main windows. The man with the loud-hailer was giving urgent warnings in Hebrew for everyone to lie down, but some jumped to their feet. In the darkness, unable to know whether they were terrorists or not, the Israelis opened fire. Among those who fell were Pasco Cohen and the Moroccan-born Jean-Jacques Maimoni. In the dim light the slim, dark-skinned youth had the look of a Palestinian. He had just fallen asleep when the sound of gunfire awakened him. He rose to his feet, barely awake, and died instantly.

Outside, the Ugandan soldiers were beginning to regroup and open fire on the men around the vehicles, whilst on the roof Yoni was leading an assault on the detachment of soldiers occupying the terrace. The Israelis who had entered the main hall below left the hostages and climbed the stairs to the second floor, in support of their commander. For the next ten minutes the fighting was fierce around the building and on the roof terrace, but the Ugandans, in spite of their superior numbers, were no match for the deadly accuracy of the Uzis in the hands of the Israeli soldiers.

The hastily re-formed Ugandan units fled into the night, while Colonel Netanyahu and his men descended from the roof terrace, now littered with dead and wounded Ugandans. On the tarmac, beside the entrance to the terminal, the communications man was keeping up a constant flow of information to the command post above, which was in turn being passed down to General Dan Shomron on the other side of the airfield.

Yoni checked his men and found only a few minor casualties, who were already being treated by the doctors from the Hercules. He informed General Adam in the Boeing above that the terminal was now secure and he was about to begin evacuating the hostages. He was stepping away from the building, moving towards the men beside the vehicles, when a Ugandan soldier hidden in the control tower took aim and fired at the figure of authority on the tarmac below.

The bullet took the commander in the back, killing him instantly. One of the doctors rushed forward, but there was nothing he could do. Israelis with bleak faces were already racing for the control tower as the doctor spoke briefly into the transmitter.

'Yoni's hit.'

Chapter 15

Defence Minister Shimon Peres was sitting in his office in the Ministry of Defence in Tel Aviv when the brief, emotionless words came through the loudspeaker.

'Yoni's hit.'

No one moved or said a word. Premier Yitzhak Rabin, with the Foreign Minister, Yigal Allon, was sitting in the office, every nerve taut as they tried to assess the constant flow of information coming from the command post above Entebbe. They both knew what would be the effect of those words on Shimon Peres.

Lieutenant-Colonel Netanyahu was one of Israel's most outstanding young officers. He had also been a close friend of the Minister of Defence who had watched his progress with pride and regarded him with deep affection. Since the attack had begun on the old terminal, Shimon Peres had been dreading the casualty reports, knowing that Yoni would be at the front of

155

anything that happened over there. Now, with only two words to grasp at, he told himself that these must mean that the commander was wounded. If that was the case he would already be back on the aircraft, receiving medical attention. Only forty minutes later, when the Hercules was in the air again, was he able to establish that Yoni Netanyahu was dead.

They had begun to gather in the Kiryah an hour earlier, leaving various functions in the city with casual apologies about other engagements. Along the corridor, in the Military Headquarters, the generals had also been gathering.

For General Mordechai Gur it was the moment of truth. After planning for every eventuality, all the decisions had been taken. Now he had to face the hardest time of all. In his office were some ten generals and senior officers who had led the tactical planning teams which had finally put together the operation now in progress. They breathed a collective sigh of relief when the C130s turned inland over Ethiopia, for this had always been the phase of the operation which could have turned into disaster. Agents at Entebbe reported no military alert as the aircraft began their final approach.

One of the generals in that room was a man who had lost a son in the Yom Kippur war. Now his second son was on his way to Entebbe in one of the C130s. A friend, aware of this, asked how he felt as his son approached the target. Before he could reply, General Gur had risen to his feet with stern, angry features.

'How can your son be in this operation?' he asked. 'You have already lost a son in the Yom Kippur and the regulations are very clear. Your second son must not be placed in the front line.'

The general rose stiffly to his feet and answered coldly. 'It is not the fault of my son that there has been a tragedy in my house. He has a right to go.'

General Gur gazed at the general for a moment, then sat down and never mentioned the subject again.

When the task force touched down at the airport the tension had built up to an almost unbearable degree. The link with Entebbe was a carrier wave that hissed and crackled, sometimes fading so that voices were lost. After the first minute the waiting generals and ministers knew that the trick had worked and that Yoni's men were already in the terminal, but even as this fact was registering they were getting reports of General Shomron's attack on the new terminal and control tower. There was fierce fighting on this side of the airfield, for there had been no element of surprise in that part of the attack.

After fifteen minutes, casualties were still

incredibly low. Although Yoni had been hit, other casualties in his force were minor, and this had been the area where they had expected the heaviest losses.

Along the corridor, in Shimon Peres's office, the static was getting worse and the three ministers were becoming increasingly frustrated. Shimon Peres finally could take it no longer. He rose to his feet and led Rabin and the Foreign Minister along the corridor into what was always considered a purely military preserve. On this night protocol went by the board and they joined General Gur and his staff in a tight, tense group around the loudspeakers.

Although there was an open line between General Gur and his second-in-command, General Adam, he left the running of the battle to his men in the field. But the minutes seemed to last for ever and there was still no word of the Migs. Unless the control tower was taken and the Migs destroyed, Shomron's force would never get off the ground.

Chapter 16

Dan Shomron's men were in action exactly forty-five seconds after the Hercules had touched down on Entebbe's main runway. Even as the pilots were reversing the turbo-props and braking the lumbering giants, the flight engineer was lowering the cargo ramps. Both aircraft came to a stop on the edge of the huge parking apron adjacent to the new terminal building. The wheels had barely stopped moving before command cars, jeeps and an armoured personnel carrier were racing down the ramps and heading for the building.

Shomrom had split his force so that they came in an arc on either side of the building, the jeeps fitted with fixed heavy calibre machine-guns which opened fire as they raced towards the building. In spite of the speed of the attack, the Ugandan soldiers on duty at the terminal had been able to recover from their initial shock and were taking up key positions in and around the building.

An air-traffic control car, commandeered by two officers who had been drinking in the lounge, made a dash for the tower. The armoured car, cutting across the tarmac, paused in its race for the terminal. The heavy machine-gun chattered briefly and the traffic control car shuddered, swerved and crashed into the side of a service building. On the far side of the tarmac a fuel tanker exploded in a ball of flames, and it seemed as though every one of the windows in the terminal's main hall were shattering in sympathy with each other.

Following the command cars were more than a hundred eager commandos, their Uzis snapping angrily in the night. They moved into the terminal through the baggage bays and the loading piers, quickly taking the ground floor of the building. Ugandan soldiers on the roof, however, commanded the approaches to the control tower and this presented General Shomron with a problem.

Two of his units had already moved off across the airfield: one to join up with Israeli agents on the road from the Ugandan Army camp, the other to begin laying explosive charges which would put the Mig fighters out of action. Shomron needed to take the control tower quickly, for it was still possible that the Ugandan technicians could contact Kampala with radio equipment in the tower.

Moving his men into position around the building, he ordered the armoured car to lay down a blistering barrage on the upper terraces of the terminal, then sent in his men. They rushed across the tarmac, using all available cover and firing continuously at the upper windows. The first Israeli soldier hit the concrete stairs of the tower and started up, turning the first corner and coming face to face with a Ugandan who shot him through the chest. The Israeli fell back and was passed down to the door, then two grenades were lobbed up the stairs.

The blast rocked the tower and broke the Ugandan resistance. Within minutes the commandos were in control of the building and entering the radar room. They found three terrified operators who were taken to a safe room downstairs, then Shomron's men lobbed a handful of grenades among the equipment and closed the door.

The unit approaching the parked Mig fighters ran into heavy fire from the Ugandans on guard there. These men had been joined by others falling back from the old terminal. For fifteen minutes they fired erratically at the fleeting shadows of the commandos, forcing them to move slowly and cautiously. Then grenades, lobbed beneath one of the Mig 21s, started a fire which quickly developed into an explosion, lighting up the entire area. The Ugandans retreated, using the darkness as cover from which to pick off Israelis as they moved among the aircraft, setting their charges.

Throughout the battle for the Migs the Ugandans expected reinforcements from the army camp at any moment, but it never came. President Amin had taken the precaution of removing most of the weapons from his soldiers at the camp because of a rumour that there would be an attempted coup whilst he was in Mauritius. The soldiers, without weapons and with little to do, had spent the evening getting drunk. For ninety minutes, while the sky was lit with blazing fires and echoing to the sound of gunfire, not one soldier left the camp. If they had, they would have found the road mined and more than twenty men waiting in the bush with machine-guns.

Dan Shomron was using part of the control tower as a command post, passing messages to Yekuti Adam in the Boeing circling above. The battle for the terminal had taken forty minutes, and there was still sporadic fire from the darkness around the perimeter and the blacked-out upper floor of the main building. Shomron knew that the situation at the old terminal was good and that the hostages were already getting on board the C130, but there was a growing danger that the noise of the battle would have alerted people outside the airport and that these would contact Amin's main force in Kampala.

Shomron discussed this possibility with Adam, who told him that their agents in Kampala, who were observing the main camps of the Ugandan forces, reported no activity so far. They knew that, once the soldiers were on the move, it would take fifty minutes for them to reach Entebbe, sufficient time for the Israelis to have loaded their aircraft and taken off.

It was the fuel problem which was causing concern. The Israeli aircraft had brought their own mobile tenders and these were hooked into the fuel valves beside the runway, but refuelling was taking longer than expected and the Hercules at the old terminal was running into serious difficulty with the equipment there. Casualties were still remarkably light, but the soldier who had been shot in the control tower was in a critical condition and the doctors on the ground wanted to get him to the mobile operating theatre in Nairobi as soon as possible.

In the Boeing, General Adam was also taking into account the fact that five of the hostages had been hit, two of them fatally, and of the three wounded the elderly Pasco Cohen was in a serious condition. To continue with the refuelling could involve delays beyond the maximum permitted time of ninety minutes on the ground. Beni Peled and Yekuti Adam agreed that the risks outweighed the advantages, and Shomron was told to secure the terminal and runway for take-off.

Shomron's unit commanders were briefed on the change of plan and the men involved in the refuelling operation were told to abandon the tenders. Half a mile away the sky was lit with flames from the two squadrons of Migs which were now totally destroyed. The unit assigned to that part of the operation had withdrawn to the Hercules, leaving their wounded with the doctors, and had then moved across the tarmac to help with the mopping up of what was now only scattered pockets of resistance.

The Ugandans on the roof of the terminal and along the perimeter could only be appalled and bewildered by the destruction. The acrid smell of cordite hung over the airfield and the air shivered to the rattle of exploding cartridges and grenades as groups of determined young commandos gradually worked their way through the long, sprawling building.

A portrait of Idi Amin, resplendent in his Field Marshal's uniform, looked down on the main hall of what, by Ugandan standards, had been a luxurious modern terminal. It was now lit by smouldering fires, the floors covered with broken glass and chunks of concrete blown out of the walls and ceiling.

But it was taking valuable time and Shomron urged his men on, sending groups around the perimeter in jeeps fitted with machine-guns to surprise any Ugandans moving towards the battle. The only soldier the jeeps surprised were moving in the opposite direction with all possible speed.

Dan Shomron had a mind like a computer and as one set of facts was communicated to him he was revising and issuing new commands, the stop watch in his head clicking away the minutes to his own personal deadline which was one a.m. local time. At five minutes to one a great weight lifted from his shoulders as across the airfield, from the old runway, a giant Hercules thundered up into the sky. It was a moment when every Israeli soldier paused and gave silent thanks that their journey had not been in vain.

Chapter 17

Fifty-three minutes earlier the one hundred and four hostages and the twelve members of the French airbus crew had suddenly found themselves in a nightmare world of fear and violence. The first burst of gunfire had occurred 150 yards beyond the terminal when most people were asleep. The Davidson family, playing cards, glanced up in alarm. A man beside them grimaced and said that some idiot Ugandan had pressed the trigger by mistake. But almost immediately there was a tremendous outburst of gunfire. Even then people in the room were trying to explain it away by saying that the other guards must have opened fire in reply to the first.

There was the thump of a grenade going off, then the steady chatter of machine-guns, and suddenly everyone knew that this was no accident. Women and children began to scream, whilst men with battle experience shouted for everyone to lie down. Bullets were cracking through the air above their heads, ricocheting off walls.

'Get down,' men shouted. 'Hit the floor.'

Even as they were doing this, to the complete astonishment of the people in the hall, there were voices on the tarmac outside; voices calling in Hebrew: *'Tishkavu, tishkavu.'*

Aryeh Brolsky, a man who understood all too well the dangers they must now face, grabbed his two daughters aged six and ten and covered them with his body. His wife was beside him and he tried to hold her in the darkness, but as the fighting came closer and the room was filled with the sound of machine-guns, she panicked and raised her head. Almost immediately she was hit and slumped unconscious beside him. In the darkness, with deafening gunfire all around, Aryeh could only clutch his children beneath him and pray.

Across the room Ilan Hartuv watched Boese appear in the doorway, slapping a magazine into his gun, gazing towards them for an interminable moment, then rushing back along the passage.

Around the room men were clutching terrified wives and children, some piling mattresses over their families. All the lights were going out on the tarmac outside and people began to shout in panic, trying to locate friends and relatives.

Akiva Lexer, the lawyer, looked up at the window as a soldier jumped on to the ledge and hung there, like some 'incredible angel', calling to them to be calm and lie down. But some were too bewildered to follow this advice.

Jean-Jacques Maimoni awoke to a terrifying world of noise and sprang to his feet. Uzi machine-guns chattered across the room and he fell, dying. The sounds and the terror were too much for Mrs Ida Borowitz. She jumped to her feet, in spite of the attempts of people around her to keep her on the floor, and became an immediate target in the dim light. She had no way of knowing that the Israeli soldiers believed there were terrorists in the room capable of raining death on the helpless people around them. So Mrs Borowitz, a moving shadow in the darkness, died without realizing that the impossible rescue had begun.

The Davidson family, with chaos all about them, crawled into the washroom and huddled there. They had not heard the shouts in Hebrew from outside the terminal, and Sarah was sure that this was the thing she had dreaded most of all, the systematic execution of the hostages.

Inside the main hall Pasco Cohen was lying in the darkness in a pool of blood, critically wounded. He had jumped to his feet when the

168

firing began in an attempt to reach his family, but neither they nor his friends knew this. As the firing continued outside, the man who had survived the death camps and all the wars of Israel was fighting his last battle.

For Nadia Israel, clutching at her young aunt in the darkness, the deafening explosions of grenades and the chattering of sub-machine-guns seemed to be everywhere. She became numbed by fear and the conviction that death would come at any moment, ceased to be aware of time or even the existence of the terminal. She retreated into a limbo of the mind and would not emerge until sanity returned around her.

The confusion continued in the terminal. At the height of the firing many of the hostages still believed that the battle was between Ugandan soldiers and terrorists. Akiva Lexer remembered the words of President Amin who had promised a solution to their problem earlier that evening. He had almost made up his mind that this must be the solution he had referred to, when an Israeli soldier with a loud-hailer began to shout through the window in Hebrew, telling everyone to be calm and lie down.

The room became quiet, many of the people stunned by the realization that this was a rescue operation. Above them, on the roof terrace, there was fierce fighting. The rattle of machine-guns was punctuated by the crack of exploding grenades. The building shook, plaster falling from the ceiling.

After more than ten minutes there was a lull in the firing and a few people risked looking out of windows. In the dim light outside they saw Israeli soldiers moving in and out of shadows, crouching around the vehicles halfway across the tarmac. Beyond them the night sky was lit with an explosion on the far side of the airfield, and in the distance they could hear a major battle in progress.

Baruch Gross was in a side room with his wife, Ruth, and son, Shy. From his window he could see the body of Wilfred Boese, sprawled beside the entrance to the terminal. Beyond it were other bodies, but even as he watched there was another flurry of gunfire from the rear of the building and he crouched down on the floor again. The firing continued for fifteen minutes, diminishing finally to occasional shots, then the Israeli soldiers began moving into the room, speaking urgently to the terrified hostages lying on the floor.

'Come quickly,' they said. 'It is time to leave. Everyone come quickly.'

The Davidson family were huddled together in the darkness of the washroom. It had been quiet for more than a minute and Sarah Davidson was beginning to believe that perhaps, after all, they would survive. Suddenly the door beside her opened and she looked up to see a young Israeli soldier looking down at her and smiling broadly. He seemed no more than a boy, and as her mouth fell open in amazement he asked in a quiet, very calm voice: 'Are you all right?'

'Yes,' she said weakly. 'But what are you doing here?'

'We've come to take you home.'

'Home!' She stared at him as though he was mad. 'How can you take us home?'

The young Israeli commando grinned. 'In an aeroplane, of course.'

At that moment Sarah Davidson wanted to kiss this young boy more than anything else in the world. Instead, like so many of the bewildered people in the terminal, she simply nodded her head and rose to her feet, then gathered her children and began walking towards the door.

Outside they saw everyone milling around, moving down the passage and on to the tarmac. Many people were only half-dressed, others dazed and having to be led by friends. There seemed to be Israeli soldiers everywhere now, talking quietly, telling people to keep calm.

Nadia Israel and her aunt were among the

first to reach the passage. Outside there was more firing and Nadia flinched, holding back, but a soldier appeared beside her and gave an encouraging grin. Ahead, just beyond the door, was a Land-Rover and she ran with her aunt towards it. People were scrambling into the vehicle, some crying, others clutching at it as though this was their only link with reality. By the time Nadia reached it the vehicle was crammed with people, but the driver slapped the bonnet and told her to climb on. She threw herself on to it, holding the bonnet with her hands, looking at the young Israeli commando with bewildered disbelief. He smiled in reassurance, then drove across the tarmac until the huge Hercules loomed up out of the darkness.

As she tumbled off the Land-Rover, clutching at her aunt's hand, she saw people running out of the night from the terminal. There were doctors by the ramp, helping people on board, asking them if they had any injuries. Inside there were soldiers, some of them cheerful, but others with bloody bandages and gaunt faces. She stumbled up the ramp and into the body of the Hercules, finding a canvas seat and sitting there with shaking hands. 'We're going home,' someone said. But even now she knew it couldn't possibly be true.

The soldiers had set up a defensive circle, their weapons pointing out into the darkness as the groups of hostages ran towards the aircraft. Some were trying to locate members of their family even as they ran, others sobbed with fear as shots rattled out across the terminal.

One child, a small boy, was being led by his mother when a burst of gunfire broke out. With a scream of fear he tore himself free and stood in the middle of the tarmac with his hands over his eyes. A young Israeli soldier moved forward, gesturing for his mother to run for the plane, then scooped the child up in his arms and started after her. From the darkness there was a burst of firing and he turned, shielding the boy with his body, firing the Uzi from his hip.

All around the terminal Israeli commandos were moving through the night like cats, waiting for the slightest sign of snipers or advancing Ugandans. Others were using Galil assault rifles fitted with night sights, constantly searching the darkness. Beyond them, from the terminal, the hostages streamed in a bewildered column.

Mrs Jocelyn Monier emerged from the main hall with blood pouring down from a shrapnel wound in her thigh. She was picked up by one soldier and placed on the back of another, who took her across to the aircraft at a jogtrot. When she arrived a doctor began treating her immediately, assuring her that it was a flesh wound and not serious.

Nili Ben-Dor, the wife of the Israeli footballer, had not even had time to dress and ran for the Hercules in her bra and briefs. She was not aware of it until she was inside the aircraft where an Israeli soldier, with a sympathetic look, took off his shirt and gave it to her.

By the time the Davidsons reached the aircraft most of the firing had stopped. They climbed up the ramp and moved along the crowded fuselage, taking seats and only then beginning to relax. Their son, Benji, still had the hand of bridge in his pocket. He showed it to Sarah who stared at it for a moment, then burst into tears. She was crying for the first time since they arrived in Entebbe . . . and she knew she should be laughing.

In the terminal Israeli commandos searched every room until they were satisfied that all the hostages had left. The bodies of Jean-Jacques Maimoni and Ida Borowitz were carried out to the aircraft, together with Pasco Cohen who was already receiving emergency treatment from a doctor. Even then it was clear that there was little hope for him.

On the aircraft soldiers counted and recounted the hostages until they were satisfied that everyone was on board. Then the Land-Rovers came up the ramp with the last of the soldiers who would travel on this aircraft.

Along the runway other commandos were spreading out, weapons sweeping the darkness in case of any attempt to fire on the Hercules as it took off. The huge aircraft taxied to the end of the old runway, switched on its lights and the turboprops roared. Within seconds it was rolling forward, gathering speed, lifting off up into the night.

It had been on the ground for just fifty-three minutes.

On the other side of the airfield, Dan Shomron set about the complicated task of withdrawing his men. Here the aerial command post was invaluable, contacting each unit over the entire area of the airport and co-ordinating the embarkation. It was a complex, time-consuming operation, but in twenty minutes all Shomron's units were around the aircraft.

The remaining Ugandan soldiers at Entebbe were in disarray. The main terminal and control tower were a shambles, the two squadrons of Mig 21s and 17s totally destroyed and still blazing. The old terminal was littered with the bodies of terrorists and Ugandans and in the darkness more than a hundred wounded soldiers were waiting for help. An armoured column, on its way from Kampala, was still thirty minutes from Entebbe.

On the runway a C130 prepared to leave. Each unit was checked on board, the vehicles ascending the ramps with the heavy armoured car the last to enter, its machine-guns ready to fire until the last moment before the ramp finally closed. Commanders checked their men, then the Hercules started down the runway and lifted into the sky.

The last aircraft was Shomron's, its ramp closing only when its sister aircraft had vanished into the night. Ugandan soldiers were beginning to advance on the runway, realizing that the attacking force was leaving. In the control tower a Ugandan officer watched the huge aircraft thunder along the runway, and as a last resort cut off the airfield runway lights.

The pilot of the Hercules, faced with total blackness, guided the aircraft by instinct, watching the air speed indicator approaching take-off speed. At one point the C130 swerved dangerously close to the edge of the runway, but the pilot brought it back, Then it was airborne and they were safe.

Over Lake Victoria, some five hundred feet above the water, a Hercules flew towards Nairobi. Inside the cargo hold was the gleaming black Mercedes which had played such a crucial role in the assault on Entebbe. To take it back to Israel was a calculated risk, for the IDF were determined to keep this aspect of their operation secret. There had been a contingency in the plan to drop the car into Lake Victoria from the C130, a relatively simple task as the cargo hold could open in flight, but the ruse had worked so perfectly that the car was now as much a part of history as the operation itself.

Less than a week before the Model 60 Mercedes, type 220, painted black, had been rusting in a junk yard three miles north of Tel Aviv. It had been found and purchased by an army supply officer whose instructions had been to find that precise model, preferably black. The car had been taken to an IDF maintenance unit where the engine had been serviced, the car resprayed and equipped with a new set of tyres. The total cost had been less than £200, and yet now it could well be priceless.

There was no doubt in the minds of the generals that one day this particular Mercedes would take its place in a military museum. For that reason they decided not to jettison the car, but to take it back to Sharm el-Sheikh where it would remain until such time as the government decided to unveil the key to operation Entebbe. In the weeks and months that followed many fanciful stories would no doubt be written about it, but the Mercedes would remain the property of the army to whom it belonged.

Chapter 18

As the C130s thundered towards Nairobi, Beni Peled and Yekuti Adam were sending their last messages to Israel before turning to follow the Hercules.

At Military Headquarters in Tel Aviv, the message brought jubilation to the generals and ministers. The 95 minutes of tension would be something they would never forget; now that it was over they could hardly bring themselves to believe that all had gone so perfectly. The operation had succeeded better than their wildest dreams, and even now it was difficult to absorb the fact that they had accomplished the impossible.

There were no speeches, no congratulations. The exhilaration of knowing was enough. In General Gur's office men who had fought a hundred campaigns were lost for words. They could only grin at each other and say: 'We did it'. One man put it more fervently. 'Tonight the Lord was with the army.'

Champagne was found and for the next hour they drank toasts to 'Shomron's guys', to the hostages, to the IDF and even to President Amin. As their spirits soared, Shimon Peres beckoned to Colonel 'Borka' Bar-Lev and took him along the corridor to his office. Closing the door he grinned and said: 'Let's phone Idi'.

Colonel Bar-Lev had spoken frequently to the Ugandan President during the week and once he got through to the palace he was quickly connected to Amin's private phone. With Shimon Peres listening on an extension, the colonel could barely control his laughter as an irritated President Amin came on the line.

'Who is this?' he asked.

'It's Borka Bar-Lev, Idi. How are you feeling?'

'Borka, it is the middle of the night!' the Ugandan President said angrily. 'Why are you calling me in the middle of the night?'

Colonel Bar-Lev began to realize that President Amin knew nothing of the attack on Entebbe. Speaking slowly, in English, he told him:

'Sir, I want to thank you for your co-operation, and I thank you very much.'

'Co-operation?' asked the President. 'You know I did not succeed.'

'No, sir, you did not. Thank you very much for your co-operation.'

179

'Have I done anything at all?' asked a bewildered Amin.

Shimon Peres, stifling his laughter, kept moving between the extension and Colonel Bar-Lev, whispering questions for him to ask.

'Ask him if we woke him up?'

Bar-Lev asked the question, but President Amin still failed to understand, telling him that the phone call had woken him. 'Why did you say I co-operated?'

'I did exactly what you wanted.'

'Wh-Wh-What happened?' Amin asked, nervously.

'What happened?' the colonel said, sounding astonished that he did not know.

'Yes?' said the President.

Bar-Lev paused, then said: 'I don't know.'

'Can't you tell me?' Amin pleaded.

'No. I don't know. I have been requested to thank you for your co-operation.'

'Can you tell me about the suggestion you made,' persisted Amin.

'I don't know what was meant by it,' Bar-Lev said and thanked him once again.

They finally said goodnight to the President and collapsed with laughter, realizing that Amin's officers were still too afraid to tell him what had happened at Entebbe. The President's men knew him too well and were under no illusions as to the fate which would await the man who first broke the news. At that time, with their spirits soaring, the Israelis were not to know of the death and persecution that would follow in the wake of President Amin's rage.

The celebrations at the Kiryah lasted all night, whilst high above the Red Sea two squadrons of Phantoms fell into position above the C130s and Boeings returning to Israel.

'*Shalom*,' said a pilot. 'Welcome home.'

In the cramped hold of a Hercules below, the rescued hostages slept or sat in silence, drained of all emotion. Many of them were still unable to comprehend what had really happened, something so incredible that it would take hours, perhaps days, to take in.

Looking at the tired young soldiers in that plane it was hard to believe that they had come all the way from Israel to bring them home. How they had done it was, at that moment, beyond their comprehension.

One of the soldiers, in an attempt to cheer them up, grinned and said: 'Listen, you don't know what you're in for when we get back. Since you went away, we've got VAT!'

Some of the hostages smiled, others groaned in mock horror. But none of them knew, not even the soldiers, what was really waiting for them. They could not know that already Ben

181

Gurion Airport in Tel Aviv was a jostling mass of deliriously happy people, overflowing from the terminal and terraces down the streets and around the fences. That people all over Israel were hugging total strangers, shouting the news again and again to anyone who would listen.

The hostages going home were oblivious to the fact that they were already a part of history, that this, the most daring exploit in modern times, would make any future hijacker pause and remember.

Inside that C130, high above the Red Sea, they were not to know that all over the world Jews were going to wake up that morning and feel ten feet tall.

Index

183